WAR RECORDS OF THE 24th PUNJABIS
(4TH BATTALION 14TH PUNJAB REGIMENT)
1914—20

[Photo: Lafayette.

LIEUT.-GENERAL SIR SKIPTON CLIMO, K.C.B., D.S.O.

WAR RECORDS

of the

24TH PUNJABIS

(4th BATTALION 14th PUNJAB REGIMENT)

1914—20

The Naval & Military Press Ltd

Reproduced by kind permission of the Central Library,
Royal Military Academy, Sandhurst

Published by
The Naval & Military Press Ltd
Unit 10, Ridgewood Industrial Park,
Uckfield, East Sussex,
TN22 5QE England
Tel: +44 (0) 1825 749494
Fax: +44 (0) 1825 765701
www.naval-military-press.com
www.military-genealogy.com

© The Naval & Military Press Ltd 2010

The Naval & Military Press ...

...offer specialist books for the serious student of conflict. The range of titles stocked covers the whole spectrum of military history with titles on uniforms, battles, official histories, specialist works containing Medal Rolls and Casualties Lists, and numismatic titles for medal collectors and researchers.

The innovative approach they have to military bookselling and their commitment to publishing have made them Britain's leading independent military bookseller.

In reprinting in facsimile from the original, any imperfections are inevitably reproduced and the quality may fall short of modern type and cartographic standards.

FOREWORD

The preparedness for war of the Army in India, so far as its officers and men were concerned, was due almost entirely to the system of training inaugurated by Lord Kitchener, ably seconded by his Chief of the General Staff, Sir Douglas Haig. The association of these two great soldiers with the Indian Army was of the happiest and was the main factor in raising all classes, of which the Indian Army is composed, to a higher standard and to a more general level of efficiency than had obtained previously.

During that vital period 1902-1914 notable and satisfactory features were the endeavours on the part of the British officers to perfect their powers of command, the pride of all ranks in their profession and in their corps, and the practical interest taken in the work and play of the Indian ranks.

These were the factors which led to each unit of the Indian Army entering the war with no inconsiderable confidence in themselves, with a sense of superiority over their opponents, and some curiosity, but little uncertainty, as to how they would comport themselves in the great struggle ahead. As to ourselves, the old 24th Punjabis, many regiments, our friends in the Punjab and our more distant comrades in the other Presidencies, may have equalled, but none, I believe, surpassed us in military spirit or practical endeavour. But of all the factors which were to stand the Regiment in such good stead I think the greatest was the exceptional quality of the junior British officers, who had joined the Regiment between 1904 and the outbreak of war. In this respect no battalion could have been more fortunate. It was due largely to their example that the Indian officers and other ranks had responded so well to the calls on their loyalty and sense of duty, and had achieved a high standard of efficiency.

It is sad to reflect that the majority of these youthful officers of such great promise were sacrificed in the early days of the war. I often wonder how far my prophesies for their future would have come true had they survived. I will close with the hope that should our Empire be brought face to face with war in the future, the 24th Punjabis may possess just such a gallant and efficient band of British and Indian Officers and Indian ranks of all classes.

S. H. CLIMO, *Lieut.-General.*
Colonel 4th Bn. 14th Punjab Regiment
(late 24th Punjabis).

Folkestone,
26th September, 1933.

CONTENTS

		PAGE
FOREWORD	... ...	v
AUTHOR'S NOTE	... ...	xi
CHAPTER I.	THE SUEZ CANAL	1
„ II.	THE BATTLE OF SHAIBA AND OPERATIONS IN THE AHWAZ AREA	4
„ III.	THE NASIRIYA OPERATIONS, 1915	12
„ IV.	THE BATTLE OF CTESIPHON AND RETREAT TO KUT ...	25
„ V.	THE SIEGE OF KUT	39
„ VI.	THE BATTALION IN CAPTIVITY	48
„ VII.	RE-FORMING THE BATTALION—MESOPOTAMIA, 1917-18—THE BATTLE OF KHAN BAGHDADI—SALONIKA	59
„ VIII.	THE BLACK SEA AND TURKEY—RETURN TO INDIA	69
APPENDICES	... ...	79-84

LIST OF ILLUSTRATIONS AND MAPS

LIEUT.-GENERAL SIR SKIPTON CLIMO, K.C.B., D.S.O.	*Frontispiece*
	FACING PAGE
BRITISH AND INDIAN OFFICERS, OCTOBER, 1914	3
THE FIGHTING NEAR SHAIBA	10
OPERATIONS IN THE AKAIKA CHANNEL, JUNE 27TH TO JULY 5TH, 1915	14
OPERATIONS NEAR NASIRIYA, JULY 6TH TO 24TH, 1915	24
THE BATTLE OF CTESIPHON	38
THE DEFENCE OF KUT-EL-AMARA, DECEMBER, 1915, TO APRIL, 1916	46
SOUTH-WESTERN ASIA	58
THE ACTION OF KHAN BAGHDADI, MARCH 26TH, 1918	64
OPERATIONS ON THE EUPHRATES LINE, MARCH, 1918	68
LOWER MESOPOTAMIA	74

AUTHOR'S NOTE

In 1925, when Lieut.-Colonel C. W. Johnston Smith, D.S.O., took over command of the 24th Punjabis (or the 4th Battalion 14th Punjab Regiment, as the Regiment was then, and is now, named), he soon realized that the " Digest of Services " for the period 1914-20 was for all practical purposes non-existent. There were only a few war diaries and reports of some of the earlier battles in which the Regiment had taken part: and these had not been co-ordinated into a connected story. He, therefore, asked me to write up the history of the Regiment for the early part of the war up to the fall of Kut. It was soon apparent that the available war diaries, reports, etc., were not suitable, in their existing form for inclusion in the Digest of Services; and I therefore undertook the task of attempting to write the history of the 24th during the whole period 1914-20. Although the account was originally written for the Digest of Services, it has been considered advisable to print it for private circulation.

If the cost of copies of the book is not put unduly high there must inevitably be a financial loss on the printing of a small publication of this description, which will only be of interest to a very limited number of individuals. The present Commandant, Lieut.-Colonel C. H. Jackson, has agreed to the loss being borne by regimental funds at his disposal, and this alone has made possible the publication of the book.

The earlier chapters are based on war diaries, reports and personal recollections, supplemented and checked by the official history. I am indebted to Brigadier J. L. Furney and Lieut.-Colonel A. C. H. Trevor for additions and for verifying the facts, and also to Captains G. P. T. Dean and P. E. C. J. Gwyn for accounts of the Regiment's work in 1919-20.

A. B. HAIG, *Brigadier.*
Commandant 4th/14th Punjab Regiment
1930-32.

1933.

CHAPTER I.

The Suez Canal.

The outbreak of the Great War found the 24th Punjabis stationed at Nowshera. The prospects of going on service appeared gloomy to the majority of officers who thought, in common with many others, that the war could only last six months and that it was unlikely that battalions would be removed from frontier stations. Only two officers happened to be at home on leave: Lieutenant Thornhill, who was retained at first with the new armies and subsequently joined the 129th Baluchis in France; and Lieutenant Langhorne who returned to India in the crowded s.s. *Dongola*. However, to everyone's joy, at 7 p.m. on October 11th, 1914, orders were received warning the 24th Punjabis for service. All mobilization measures were started at once, so that by the 22nd the depot had been organized and housed in separate barracks, all surplus kit stored and Major Cooke sent to the reserve centre at Jhelum to collect and select the reservists who were beginning to assemble.

On October 24th orders were received that the 24th Punjabis were allotted to the 30th Indian Infantry Brigade, part of Indian Expeditionary Force " F " which was originally destined for service in France but which was eventually detained in Egypt. On the next day 75 reservists joined from Jhelum, so that on October 26th the Regiment was able to parade complete with the exception of 70 rank and file who were to come from the 19th Punjabis and 25 reservists who had still to come from Jhelum. These latter arrived on October 28th. Orders for the move to Karachi were received on October 27th and the Regiment left Nowshera on the morning of the 30th, arriving at Kiamari docks at 7.30 a.m. on November 2nd. Embarkation on the H.T. *Takada* of the B.I.S.N. Company commenced immediately and was finished by 12 noon except for reserve ammunition which was all on board at 1 p.m. The *Takada* left dock at 10.15 p.m. for the stream and sailed at 6.30 a.m. next day with nine other transports, escorted by H.M.S. *Duke of Edinburgh*. The convoy was formed in two lines of five ships each, an escorting ship being ahead and between the two lines. The H.T. *Takada* led the starboard column.

The convoy arrived at Aden early on November 9th, and leaving the same day at 3 p.m. arrived at Suez on the morning of November 16th. On the 18th the Regiment commenced disembarkation, and at 3.30 p.m. marched from the docks to the camp of the 30th Infantry Brigade situated in the desert on the far side of Suez Town, and some four miles from Port Tewfik.

The next day No. 1 Double Company and the Machine Gun Section under Major Morton and Lieutenant Birbeck moved in barges up the canal to relieve The Highland Light Infantry at El Shatt post, and were in turn relieved on November 20th by the 126th Baluchistan Infantry. The active work of the 24th Punjabis may, therefore, be said to begin from this date. As a test of the efficiency of the Regiment the timing of a practice entrainment may be of interest. This was held on December 2nd. The personnel was entrained in 46 minutes from the time that the surprise order was given; and the 1st Line transport consisting of 36 pack mules and 13 A.T. carts took 1 hour and 18 minutes. The time taken to detrain and load the transport was one hour.

The 30th Infantry Brigade under the command of Major-General C. J. Melliss, V.C., C.B., and composed of the 24th and 76th Punjabis, 126th Baluchistan Infantry and 2nd/7th Gurkha Rifles, were holding the Suez section of the canal defences, *i.e.*, from Port Tewfik to the Little Bitter Lake (exclusive). The defences were mostly on the west bank but some posts were sited on the east bank. Actually, one battalion and a half were in outposts on the east bank. A military bridge was erected in this section at El Kubri, but had to be continually dismantled to allow traffic to pass through the canal. The whole defence system of the canal was held by three Indian Brigades, and the dispositions as a whole excited comment as the line of the canal was the main line of defence; while, in the opinion of many, the main line should have been well forward on the east bank so as to protect the canal and to allow traffic through it. Our operations at this period were very much of a defensive character: we allowed the Turks to reconnoitre the desert between Egypt and Palestine and to cross it later at their leisure.

On December 24th the 24th Punjabis took over the outposts, the brigade outposts being under the command of Lieut.-Colonel Climo. The remainder of the brigade was employed in digging defences chiefly on the west bank and in preparing for an attack. Part of the Bikanir Camel Corps, sixty strong, joined the sector, and Major Rawlins, 24th Punjabis, who commanded the camel corps, came in person. H.H. the Aga Khan also visited the Regiment on the 27th.

The first serious report of the enemy's presence was received on January 23rd, 1915. An aeroplane reported enemy shelters on the east of the Lesser Bitter Lake, while on the 25th an aeroplane reported the presence of 5,000 enemy and four guns near Bir Mabeuik, ten miles from the canal. The enemy did not, however, appear in such force. On the night of January 26th-27th they approached No. 2 Post midway between El Shatt and El Kubri, and El Kubri itself, but were discovered by our infantry patrols. The enemy were estimated by Major Cooke, in command of No. 2 Post, at 100 men. They advanced to within 300 yards of the post, and from about 0300 hours to 0430 hours intermittent fire was

BRITISH AND INDIAN OFFICERS : OCTOBER, 1914.

Top Row (*Left to Right*).—Jem. Sohan Singh.   Jem. Ujagar Singh.   Sub. Kishen Singh.   Capt. G. Leslie-Smith.
2nd Row (*Left to Right*).—Jem. Jhanda Singh.   Capt. R. C. Clifford, I.M.S.   Sub. Gul Akbar.   Capt. A. C. H. Trevor.   Capt. W. F. B. Edwards.   Sub. Labh Singh. Jem. Fateh Singh, I.O.M.   Lieut. D. Hobart.   Jem. Hashim Ali.   Sub. Ali Muhammad.   Lieut. C. C. Langhorne.   Lieut. M. Birkbeck.   Jem. Bhola Singh. Jem. Amir Khan.
3rd Row (*Sitting*).—Sub. Muhammad Khan, I.M.D.   Rai Sahib Jonki Pershad.   Sub. Diwan Singh.   Major H. W. F. Cooke.   Lieut.-Col. S. H. Climo, D.S.O. Sub.-Maj. Sakt Chand, Bahadur.   Major S. Morton.   Sub. Sawan Singh, I.O.M.   Capt. A. B. Haig.
4th Row (*On Ground*).—Jem. Narain Singh.   Jem. Pirthi Chand.   Lieut. E. S. Rind.   Jem. Satiazar.   Jem. Lal Khan.   Lieut. H. M. Pim.   Sub. Sahib Nur.   2/Lieut. W. I. L. Passy.

carried on. The enemy retired at 0500 hours, before dawn. The enemy left a number of haversacks, field glasses, etc., at our wire. This attack was actually the first one made by the Turks on the Canal defences, and was intended as a feint to draw attention away from the main attack, which took place two or three days later in the Toussum area. After the withdrawal of the Turkish forces a strong reconnaissance, consisting of a detachment of Hyderabad I.S. Lancers and No. 4 Double Company, under Captain Edwards went out to the site of the Turkish Camp at Bir Mabeuik. No information of value was obtained. No further alarm occurred on this sector of the Canal Defences, and the Regiment was relieved from the outposts and concentrated at Suez on February 27th. During the Regiment's stay in Suez a strong detachment was embarked on H.M.S. *Ocean* and taken down the Gulf of Suez to Tor. In this vicinity were some manganese mines, and the object of the expedition was to discover the condition of the mines which were reported to have been damaged by Turks or their agents. No Turks, however, appeared to have been there. In the first half of March rumours were prevalent of the transfer of the brigade from Suez. These rumours were eventually confirmed, and the brigade was ordered to Mesopotamia, being relieved in the Suez sector by the 28th Indian Brigade—the Frontier Force Brigade, another formation of the original I.E.F. " F."

CHAPTER II.

THE BATTLE OF SHAIBA AND OPERATIONS IN THE AHWAZ AREA.

THE Regiment accordingly embarked for Mesopotamia on March 22nd as follows:—

> 2 British officers and the Machine Gun Section on the *Kelvingrove*.
> 4 British officers, 2 Indian officers, and 86 rank and file (" E " Company) on the *Soldier Prince*.
> H.Q. and remainder on the *Chilka* (8 British officers, 17 Indian officers, 700 rank and file, and 24 followers).

The Regiment arrived at Aden on March 27th, left the next evening, and the ships arrived at Basra on April 3rd, 4th and 5th, 1915. The main portion of the Battalion disembarked from the *Chilka* on the 7th and proceeded to Makina Masus in the river steamer, *Blosse Lynch*, pitching camp in a blinding dust storm. On the 8th the machine-gun detachments and first line transport arrived, but the latter was withdrawn at once.

Orders were received at 1900 hours, April 11th, for the Regiment to hold itself in readiness to proceed to Shaiba. The Regiment thus took part in the Battle of Shaiba, an account of which follows:—

Battle of Shaiba, April 12th to 14th, 1915.

Early on April 12th the 30th Indian Infantry Brigade marched from the camp at Makina Masus to the Zobair Gate of Basra City. An attempt was made to cross on foot to Shaiba through the flooded area. The brigade took to the water at 0730 hours, but owing to the depth of the water in places, the effort was abandoned at 1330 hours, and the brigade returned to Khora Post, which was reached at 1500 hours.

The 24th Punjabis now received orders to be prepared to cross to Shaiba in bellums, and at 1545 hours these orders were confirmed. The bellum is a local boat on the lines of a Canadian canoe, capable of holding ten armed men and about 400 lb. of baggage, etc. At 1630 hours 80 bellums started, carrying the brigade staff 13 British officers, 16 Indian officers, and 572 Indian other ranks. The bellums were handled by 160 men of the 20th Punjabis. Until 1930 hours progress was easy. From that time onwards the water was shallow, consequently officers and men took to the water and pushed the boats for the remainder of the journey. The first boat arrived at Shaiba at 2100 hours, and by 2359 hours the Battalion had assembled in the Cavalry Brigade area and remained under the orders of the G.O.C. Cavalry Brigade during the night of April 12th-13th. One bellum went astray in the darkness and was evidently captured by Arabs. No news was heard of the occupants until after the fall of Kut, when the solitary survivor was found in a state of great weakness and destitution as a prisoner in the hands of the Turks.

At 0900 hours, April 13th, the Battalion came under the orders of the G.O.C. 16th Indian Infantry Brigade (Brig.-General W. S. Delamain) and took part in the operations against North Mound, in which the 24th Punjabis formed the left Battalion of the leading line, the 2nd Dorsets being in a similar position on the right.

Moving with special flank guards on the exposed (left) flank, an uninterrupted advance was made on North Mound, which was occupied at 1110 hours. Several captures of arms, etc., were effected, including an impressive green and gold standard. At 1200 hours the withdrawal was ordered. However, when about half-way back to Kiln Post orders were received to resume the advance, but in a westerly direction. In this advance the 24th Punjabis moved in echelon on the right flank of the 104th Rifles. The advance was carried out under ineffective rifle fire to within a few hundred yards of the Turkish guns, and the officers and detachments surrendered to the Regiment. The captures made by the Battalion were two breech-loading mountain guns, with one artillery officer and twelve other ranks. After this operation the force returned to the entrenched camp at Shaiba for the night, and the 24th took over a portion of the perimeter.

The Battalion moved out for operations at 0900 hours, April 14th, being again attached to the 16th Indian Infantry Brigade which was acting with the remainder of the 6th Division and Cavalry Brigade, the whole under the command of General C. J. Melliss, V.C., C.B. The strength of the Battalion was 12 British officers, 16 Indian officers, and 492 Indian other ranks.

In the initial advance to South Mound the 24th Punjabis was the right battalion of the first line; the Dorsets were the left battalion, and the 117th Mahrattas and 119th were in reserve. The 24th advanced in two lines: Nos. 2 and 3 Double Companies in the first, and Nos. 1 and 4 Double Companies in the second line, the whole being in lines of platoons in fours at fifty paces interval covered by scouts. During the initial advance the Battalion was subjected to long-range rifle and ineffective artillery fire.

After occupying South Mound the first line of the 24th Punjabis entrenched 500 yards west of it. During this halt the Cavalry Brigade and 18th Indian Infantry Brigade on the right were engaged in a heavy fire fight and bodies of hostile cavalry kept moving across our front, but outside effective rifle range. About 1145 hours Turkish artillery was directed against the reverse slope of South Mound, some of their shells bursting among the platoons but causing no damage.

About noon the advance of the 16th Indian Infantry Brigade was resumed in a south-west direction. This necessitated a partial change of front but the manœuvre was completed on the move without casualties, notwithstanding a great increase in the volume of fire. About 1220 hours the first line came under heavy and well directed fire at about 600 yards range. This compelled both forward battalions to halt. Preparations were made to open fire. Hostile fire from machine guns and rifles was sustained from points wide on the right and left as well as from the centre. Casualties became more frequent, especially in units attempting any movement. It was difficult to locate the enemy in his trenches while the mirage added considerably to the difficulty of observation.

The fact that the sound of bullets appeared to come lower as the supporting lines approached the firing line made it clear that the hostile trenches were on ground sloping downwards from our own firing line, and that the latter was on the top of an undulation which formed a sky line to the Turks. The advantage of firing up-hill was obvious. A visit to the front line demonstrated that the firing line of the 16th Indian Infantry Brigade was lying just short of the scarcely perceptible rise, and therefore could not see the Turkish front line trenches. In point of fact, the only unit directing its fire on these trenches was the Machine Gun Section, which was on the right of the Battalion and on somewhat higher ground. It was realized, therefore, that the firing line must creep forward a few yards to obtain a view of the nearest Turkish trenches.

About 1230 hours Lieutenant D. Hobart, who had been sent to the junction of the Dorsets and 24th Punjabis and who had just returned, was dangerously wounded. At the same hour a message was received from the G.O.C. 16th Indian Infantry Brigade to the effect that the Battalion was not to become seriously engaged; but before this order arrived the Battalion was involved in a severe fight within 600 yards of the enemy. The firing line now advanced to the edge of the slope which led down towards the Turkish trenches. The latter were sited 400 to 600 yards away and, being on lower ground, the Turks had the advantage of firing upwards; at the same time the trenches were out of view of our artillery observation posts and there was considerable delay in getting our guns on to the true target— the front line trenches. One disadvantage to the enemy was at once apparent, namely, that if our troops could hold this line the enemy could neither reinforce nor replace the ammunition of their advanced line, for the latter was some 1,700 yards in advance of the Barjisiya Wood where the reserves were posted, and whence it would be necessary to advance over open ground swept by our artillery, machine guns and rifle fire. No communication trenches had been prepared from rear to front.

At this stage the heat was excessive, water scarce, and the probable duration of the fire fight necessitated careful expenditure of ammunition. Between 1230 and 1430 hours the first line was gradually reinforced by the second line. There was no slackening in the enemy's fire which increased in intensity against any forward movement, with which the Turks appeared to be always ready to deal.

At 1300 hours the first line was congested with wounded. Colonel Climo therefore sent back Lieutenant Langhorne from the first line to explain the situation to the G.O.C. 16th Brigade, and to ask what the Commander's intention was. This officer was accompanied by his two orderlies and was severely wounded whilst executing this mission. No reply was received for more than two hours; in any case, no forward movement was possible as the hostile fire continued to increase in intensity until just before 1600 hours.

The Machine Gun Section had come into action on the right of the Battalion about 1230 hours and maintained its position under a particularly galling fire until it was compelled to shift its position about 1500 hours. The losses of the section amounted to ten out of eighteen. There is little doubt that the Turks had marked down its position early in the day and employed every effort to put the section out of action. The endurance exhibited by the gun teams deserves every praise, for it was due to the effective fire of the machine guns that the firing line was able to maintain its position.

Major Cooke and Captain Haig were wounded between 1430 and 1530 hours. The former was with a mixed unit of "F" and "E" Companies, and a company of the 119th Infantry, three companies of which had reinforced the battalion at 1500 hours. This portion of the line in the right centre of the Battalion had worked its way forward and was for some time in advance of the rest of the Brigade and, though losing men steadily, it held its ground. Between 1545 and 1615 hours portions of the Battalion, along its whole front, had worked forward in short rushes. In one of these Captain Edwards was killed, and about the same time Subedar Sahib Nur was mortally wounded and died before the final advance.

About 1615 hours large numbers of the enemy were seen retiring in haste from their camps in Barjisiya Wood, and somewhat later certain of those occupying supporting trenches were noticed evacuating their positions. At 1630 hours a reply came to the message to the G.O.C. 16th Brigade, to the effect that the position was to be taken. This information was passed along the line and to the units on either flank. About ten minutes later a general advance took place. In the first few yards of the 200 yards which intervened a number of casualties were occasioned by an outburst of fire from the Turkish reserve trenches. Then their fire suddenly ceased. The advance continued without a pause to the Turkish trenches which were occupied at about 1700 hours. In the front line trenches numbers of Turkish dead and wounded were found, roughly speaking two to every three yards. The survivors surrendered and large quantities of rifles and two machine guns were captured.

A peculiar manifestation revealed itself during the long period in which the firing line was held up, in that officers and men who had never been under fire previously were overcome by sleep for a period of ten to fifteen minutes. The general condition was that of alternate men sleeping while their next-door neighbour fired with slow and deliberate aim; there was a complete absence of rapid fire.

The casualties sustained in this day's fighting were: 1 British officer, 1 Indian officer, and 21 Indian other ranks killed; 5 British officers, 6 Indian officers, and 106 Indian other ranks wounded. This was equivalent to 27 per cent. of the Battalion's strength.

In addition to the award of the I.O.M. and I.D.S.M. to a number of the Indian ranks, Lieut.-Colonel Climo was promoted to Brevet-Colonel, and Jemadar Sohan Singh was awarded the Military Cross for his gallantry during the battle.

As mentioned in General Melliss's Report the battle was essentially a "soldiers' battle." When the force left Shaiba Camp it was uncertain where the enemy was. The troops moved on a broad front from the beginning, and owing to the configuration of the ground encountered the enemy at close range. Hence there was no considered plan of attack, and it was left to the grit of the troops to wear down the Turkish resistance. The result of the battle was far reaching. The Turkish threat to Basra was removed once and for all. In addition to losing over 700 prisoners the Turkish and Arab casualties in the three days' fighting are calculated to have been 5,000 to 6,000.

A special complimentary order was issued to the Battalion by Brig.-General W. S. Delamain, to whose brigade the 24th were attached during the Shaiba operations. In this order General Delamain, after expressing his admiration of the steadiness and gallantry of all ranks in the battle, stated that "the Regiment on this occasion added greatly to its already high reputation. The G.O.C. deeply regrets the loss of so many gallant comrades who fell in a successful endeavour to uphold the fine fighting traditions of the Regiment."

Complimentary orders were also received from General Melliss, commanding at Shaiba, from the Force Commander, General Sir John Nixon, and from the Viceroy and Commander-in-Chief in India.

The funeral of the late Captain W. F. B. Edwards took place in the British cemetery at 12 noon on April 15th. Nearly every British officer and numbers of the men could produce ocular evidence of narrow escapes in the form of bullet holes through head-dresses, uniforms, water-bottles, haversacks, etc., while some ten to sixteen of the wounded men were hit by more than one bullet. No. 864 Sepoy Lachman Singh, a recruit of a few months' service, was hit in three places and evinced a very cheery spirit throughout his time in hospital.

The 30th Infantry Brigade, with the exception of the 24th Punjabis, was not employed in the Shaiba operations and the Regiment remained on at Shaiba as a divisional battalion from April 15th to 18th. It is a pleasant duty to place on record the kindness and assistance rendered to all ranks of the Regiment by the 16th Cavalry and 7th Lancers; for we arrived at Shaiba with practically nothing but what we stood up in, and for a week were dependent on the charity of others, and we never felt the pinch of want.

On April 18th the Battalion marched to its old camp at Makina Masus. This was a trying ordeal. For a long seven miles of the journey the column waded through water varying in depth from 15 inches to 3 feet, while the mud and the glare off the water had a singularly exhausting effect. On arrival at camp the 76th Punjabis took forcible possession of officers and men and entertained us in a most hospitable manner. Their kindness did not end here, for with the 7th Gurkhas they had pitched our camp and brought back our heavy kit from the base depot, so that with the march the day's labour was ended.

From April 19th to 25th the days were occupied in refitting and completing equipment and in visiting our wounded. The latter was a lengthy proceeding, as the wounded were distributed over a large area of hospital sheds. The weather also was bad, heavy rain falling from 21st to 25th.

On April 26th the Regiment marched from its camp at Makina Masus to the Viceroy's pier (strength: 10 British officers, 12 Indian officers, 611 Indian other ranks, and 39 followers), where it embarked on the s.s. *Blosse Lynch* and barges and sailed shortly after noon towards the Karun River. On April 27th the Regiment disembarked at Saba, a point half-way between Mohammerah and Ahwaz, at 1700 hours, and bivouacked with the remainder of the 12th Division until the evening of the 28th, when a night march was made to a bivouac twelve miles up-stream. On the night of the 29th the march was continued parallel to the river as far as Braika, where the Division halted for two days.

On May 1st the 30th Brigade and the 7th Cavalry Brigade marched at 0400 hours northwards from the river in the direction of the old Karkha River. The absence of water delayed the selection of a bivouac. Ultimately a few shallow stretches of rain-water were found, round which some small wells were excavated and from which a sufficiency of water was procured. The following day the Brigade moved on a few miles to an old canal, in which an ample supply of excellent water was found. At this bivouac the Division assembled, and on May 6th the march was resumed to the Karkha River, which was reached at 0100 hours. After a rest of three hours the Brigade started at 0430 hours, and halted four miles farther on at Illa on the left bank of the Karkha River.

At 1100 hours on May 9th the Battalion commenced the passage of the river. This was carried out in Berthon boats, a small proportion of the heavy kit being sent across by a flying bridge. The crossing was completed by 1600 hours. The Brigade bivouac on the right bank was a pleasant contrast to the dust and flies we had experienced on the opposite side of the river. The climate was still delightful. The sun, though hot, was by no means unbearable, while the evenings and mornings were quite cool and the nights cold enough to necessitate two blankets. During these operations we had no tents nor did we find the need of them imperative, and in almost all subsequent operations tents were not taken.

On May 12th, owing to the arrival of more units from the left bank, we moved to another portion of the perimeter. Yet another move became necessary on the 13th owing to the dispatch of a flying column towards Kafajieh to deal with the Benilam tribe who had been responsible for the treacherous shooting of three cavalry officers on April 29th.

The passage of troops, horses, transport mules and supplies had necessitated heavy calls on the time and energies of the men, and work was continuous night and day throughout the twenty-four hours. On the whole, however, there were few sick. In connection with the swimming of horses a somewhat quaint expedient was tried to induce the horses to cross to the other side. The attraction was provided by the music of the combined bugle, pipe, drum and surnai bands of the 30th Brigade. The melody, though very military and calculated to draw, was not a success.

On May 16th orders were received for the march of the Battalion to Ahwaz on the following day. The return passage across the river commenced the next day at 0530 hours and was completed by 0830 hours. This constituted a record and is by no means an unsatisfactory performance for the passage of a river 220 yards in breadth with a rapid current. Twelve Berthon boats were available for personnel, while two flying bridges were available for baggage; the latter were able to take three and two tons respectively, and a trip inclusive of loading, unloading, and the return journey, occupied thirty to thirty-five minutes. The Berthon boats accommodated ten men fully armed and accoutred, of whom four formed the crew, the latter returning after each trip for which the average time worked out at twenty minutes.

At 0430 hours on May 17th the Battalion marched from Illa to Ghadir, which was reached at 1930 hours. The march was resumed at 0500 hours on the 18th, and Ahwaz reached three hours later. This was the first day of uncomfortable heat, and marked the commencement of the hot weather proper. On arrival we received orders to embark on the " P.4 " so as to be ready to sail at 1600 hours. A start was made before this hour and after steaming down-stream for three hours a halt was made until 0430 hours the next morning. Mohammerah was passed at noon, and Basra reached at 1900 hours. The Battalion commenced disembarking on the morning of May 20th and marched to Khora, where we remained in camp until June 14th. The heat and insects rendered our three weeks' rest if anything more expensive as regards casualties from sickness than if we had been engaged

To illustrate fighting near Shaiba

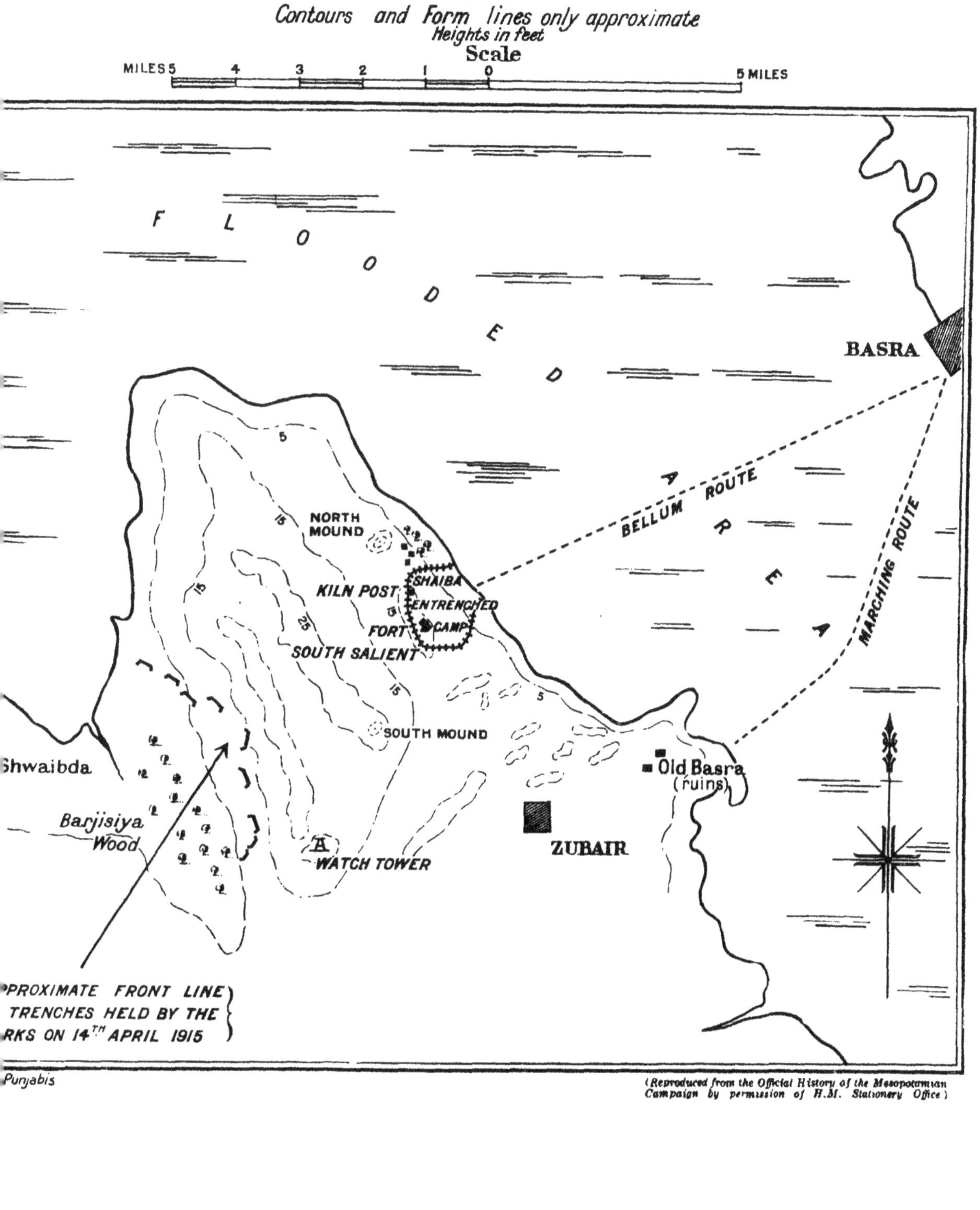

(Reproduced from the Official History of the Mesopotamian Campaign by permission of H.M. Stationery Office)

in operations. Mosquito nets and goggles were served out to every man. The former, however, were too small to be of any practical use; in consequence all units became greatly reduced by malaria.

On the 22nd Major Cooke rejoined and took over temporary command from Lieut.-Colonel Climo who had been appointed to the command of the 17th Brigade for the operations on the Tigris beyond Qurna. On May 25th a draft of reinforcements joined from the depot, consisting of 75 of our own men and 50 of the 31st Punjabis, the latter half Dogras and half P.Ms. On June 9th Lieut.-Colonel Climo rejoined on the conclusion of the operations resulting in the capture of Amara.

CHAPTER III.

The Nasiriya Operations, 1915.

On June 14th the Battalion marched from Khora at 0600 hours and embarked on the *Blosse Lynch* which sailed at 1100 hours and reached Qurna the same evening. The Battalion disembarked on the left bank of the Tigris next morning, and moved into the post at Mezerah about three-quarters of a mile inland.

The 30th Infantry Brigade was under orders to move out on a punitive expedition against the marsh Arabs on June 21st. This would have entailed fighting in water. The training of crews in handling bellums, therefore, commenced on June 15th. The Arabs, however, submitted to our terms on the 20th and the proposed operations were cancelled.

When the 30th Brigade arrived in Mesopotamia in the middle of April the 6th Indian Division was the only formation in the country. Subsequently in addition to the 30th Brigade two more brigades (the 12th and 33rd) were sent from India. These three brigades were formed into the 12th Indian Division under command of Major-General G. F. Gorringe. The 12th Division was, however, really a division in name only, for it was allotted no artillery or ancillary arms. When the 12th Division was employed the necessary artillery, sappers, etc., were borrowed from the 6th Division.

The progress of the campaign so far had resulted in the capture of Basra and Qurna, in the defeat of the Turkish attempt to recapture Basra, and in the frustration of the Turkish efforts to damage the Anglo-Persian oilfields north-west of Ahwaz. Subsequent to this, the 6th Division had advanced up the Tigris and had captured Amara. It was now the turn of the 12th Division to move up the Euphrates with the object of capturing Nasiriya.

On June 26th accordingly the Battalion embarked on the *Medjidieh* at 1700 hours and steamed up the Euphrates to concentrate with the remainder of the 30th Brigade for the impending operations in the direction of Nasiriya. On June 27th the transports reached the obstruction constructed at the junction of the Hammar Lake and the Akaika Channel, and the next seven days were occupied in passing our fleet through the obstruction. The *modus operandi* was the employment of three parties of men, numbering 200, 100 and 50 respectively, who pulled each ship through. This was trying work and affected the health and strength of the Brigade; it entailed the men being in the water for four or five hours at a stretch working under the fierce rays of the Arab sun. In addition, the men had to endure the discomfort of living cooped up in iron barges. This told adversely on the health of all ranks.

On July 3rd the *Medjidieh* passed through the obstruction at 0900 hours. So expert had the men now become that this steamer, one of the biggest of the fleet, occupied no longer than thirty minutes in negotiating the passage. The remainder of the day was spent in hauling our bellums up-stream and in re-rafting them.

On July 4th the fleet moved up to Atis House, down-stream of which we anchored about 1700 hours. A somewhat hot engagement appeared to be in progress at the time of our arrival, and a fair percentage of bullets coming over fell among the shipping. At 1800 hours operation orders were issued for the attack of the brigade on the village on the Akaika Channel. General Gorringe's intention was to advance along both banks of the Akaika Channel to its junction with the Euphrates, and to secure the left bank of the river preparatory to attacking and capturing the Turkish gun positions on the right bank of the river opposite the Akaika Channel entrance. The troops on the right or south bank of the channel were held up by a deep creek, and as will be seen from the following account the attainment of General Gorringe's objectives was mainly due to the action of the 24th Punjabis. The Regiment was to be on the right of the 76th Punjabis, and this involved an advance in bellums over water against a mud wall and village.

Engagement on the Akaika Channel, July 5th, 1915.

At 0540 hours the passage of the bellums through the cutting east of Atis House commenced, and by 0620 hours the bellums were manned by their crews and filed past the 30th Mountain Battery. At 0635 hours the Battalion advanced in three lines of double companies with the Machine Gun Section on the right. No. 3 Double Company in bellums and 100 rank and file on foot under Lieutenant Haverfield had joined the brigade reserve. Up to 0730 hours the advance proceeded under rifle and shell fire, the latter being particularly well directed. The Battalion hove to from time to time in order to correct alignment with the supporting line of the 76th Punjabis.

At 0740 hours the Battalion arrived at a point 800 yards from the long line of low walls which faced it. At this point the bellums came under a heavy burst of rifle fire and casualties occurred at once. The only remedy was, therefore, to turn the boats broadside on and to return the fire. This, combined with the fire of the Machine Gun Section, held the hostile fire more or less in check. The Battalion was now about 300 yards in rear of the right flank of the leading line of the 76th Punjabis, whose advance had been brought to a standstill.

At 0840 hours a message from the G.O.C. 30th Brigade was received ordering the Battalion to advance. A reply was sent that the Battalion would advance in bellums as soon as arrangements for covering fire were completed. But as it seemed certain that the Battalion would be annihilated in any attempt to cross the open water in bellums, Lieut.-Colonel Climo visited Brigade Headquarters and discussed the situation with the G.O.C. The latter gave the C.O. verbal orders to land the Battalion in order to support the right of the 76th Punjabis and to press forward the attack on that flank.

At 0935 hours Lieut.-Colonel Climo returned to the Battalion and ordered it to land and to form five lines, one company in each at fifty paces distance. The remaining company and the Machine Gun Section were disposed on the extreme right flank under cover, at a range of 750 yards from the line of walls with orders to cover the advance, to neutralize hostile fire from the walls, and generally to deal with any hostile action on this flank.

At 1004 hours the advance was resumed and almost immediately a message was received, timed 1000 hours, from Adjutant 76th Punjabis regarding the check to their advance. It appeared that there was a village 200 yards in front of the right of the 76th Punjabis, which was holding up the advance. A detachment under Lieutenant Haverfield had been sent to reinforce the right of the 76th Punjabis. On arrival they were ordered to attack the village. The attack was launched but was recalled by the O.C. 76th Punjabis after proceeding fifty yards.

Lieut.-Colonel Climo proceeded immediately to the leading line of the 76th Punjabis and there discussed the situation with the officer commanding that unit. Lieut.-Colonel Climo came to the conclusion that the risk of enfilade and reverse fire must be taken and the advance resumed from the right flank, first against the village and tower 200 yards in front and then up to the Euphrates.

The G.O.C. Brigade now reached the front line and ordered the 24th to press forward on the right. The advance was resumed forthwith, Lieutenant Haverfield with his detachment leading, supported by the right-half battalion under Major Morton, whose orders were to capture the village, to leave Lieutenant Haverfield's party in occupation, and himself to continue the advance up to the Euphrates. Two companies and the Machine Gun Section were to remain in position on the right flank to cover the advance. At 1045 hours the tower and village were occupied although the advance to this position had to be made through water and mud three to five feet deep.

At 1100 hours the Machine Gun Section and bellums were ordered forward. At 1145 hours the right-half battalion, after a rapid advance through deep water and under heavy enfilade rifle fire and a rain of pom-pom shells, reached the left bank of the Euphrates. The majority of casualties during this advance occurred in crossing an open piece of lagoon which was flanked from a village on the right bank of the Akaika Channel. Attackers and defenders now faced each other with a river some three hundred yards wide separating them. The arrival of the 24th Punjabis on the Euphrates' bank was the signal for a heavy burst of firing from the

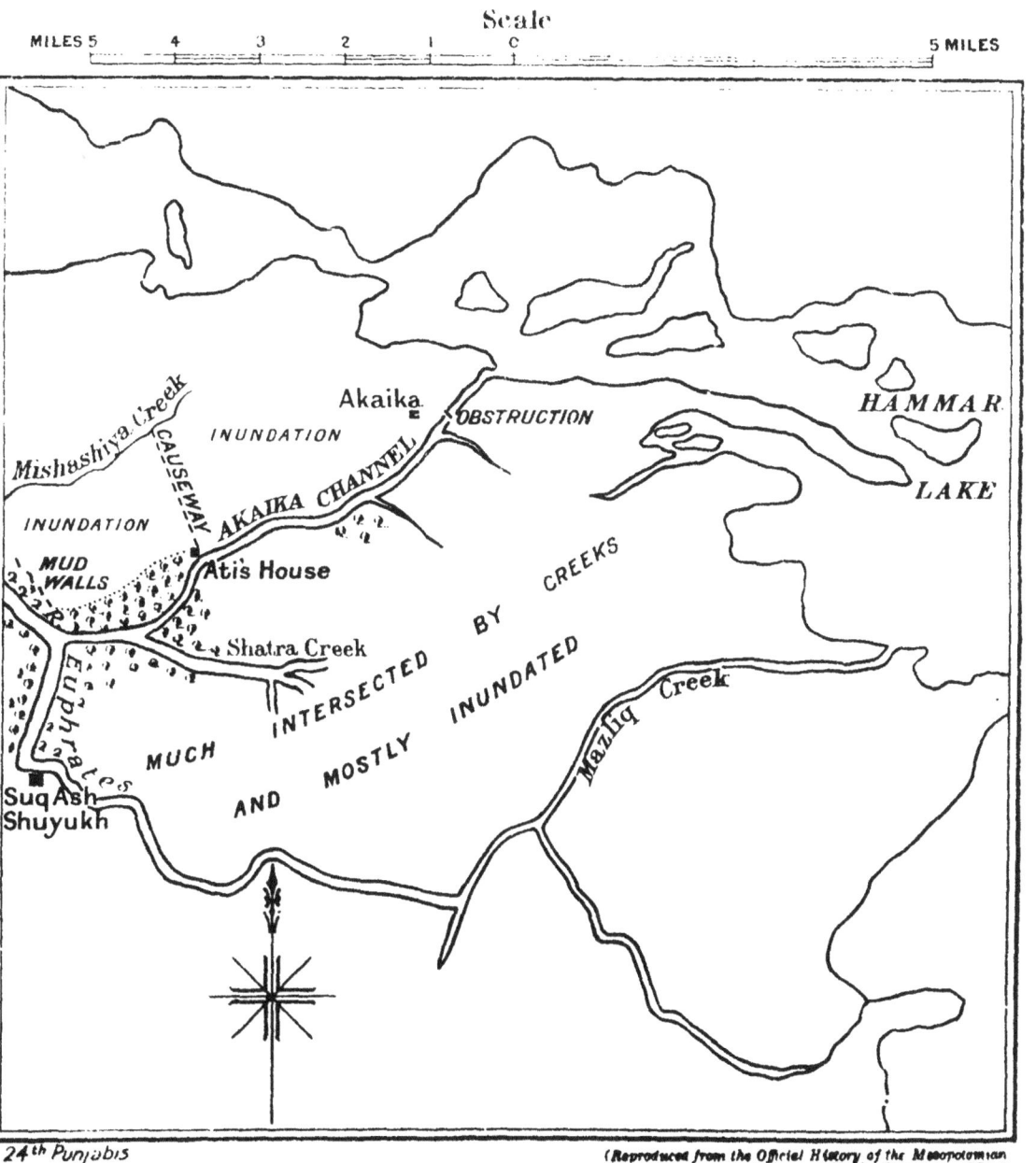

enemy main position on the opposite bank of the Euphrates. This fire continued for nearly one hour, during which period pom-poms and machine guns were brought to bear by the Turks from their steamers which had moved up-stream and were thus enfilading the left bank from the right flank. During the original advance one company had been detached to the left flank to deal with the hostile forces on the right bank of the Akaika Channel. Their presence on that flank was the main factor in enabling the advance to progress so successfully.

At 1240 hours the Machine Gun Section and a portion of the 76th Punjabis reached the Euphrates; the former came into position on our extreme right flank and were able to bring enfilade fire to bear on the Turkish gun positions and on many of the hostile infantry trenches. After enduring this for half an hour the enemy commenced to evacuate their trenches.

At 1320 hours it was evident the Turks were badly shaken. A few minutes later white flags were raised in the Turkish trenches. Fire was stopped on our side, whereupon the Turks rose and made signs of surrender. At 1325 hours the G.O.C. Brigade arrived, and orders were issued for the bellums to be passed from the lagoon into the stream of the Euphrates. This, however, was no easy matter, as the bellums, requiring some sixty men each to lift, had to be carried nearly 100 yards across the intervening strip of land. At 1400 hours the G.O.C., Brigade Major, Officer Commanding 24th Punjabis, and Adjutant with four Indian ranks crossed the river and took formal possession of the prisoners and guns.

At 1415 hours under orders of the G.O.C. half the Battalion was ordered to cross to the right bank. Outposts were disposed to the south-west and west; parties were detailed to take over and count captured arms and ammunition, and the prisoners were transferred to the left bank. By 1700 hours Battalion Headquarters and half the Battalion had crossed the river and protection for the night was completed.

The casualties were Subedar Ali Mohomed and 24 Indian other ranks wounded. The following captures were made: Two 3.9" Krupp Guns, about eight Turkish officers and 200 other ranks.

The night of July 5th–6th passed without incident. At 0500 hours on July 6th the Battalion was ordered to re-embark on the *Medjidieh;* this was completed by 0700 hours. The Divisional Commander (Major-General Gorringe) and the G.O.C. Brigade congratulated the Regiment on their behaviour on July 5th, especially on " the manner in which the final part of the advance was carried out at a critical moment of the engagement."

At 1220 hours, after transferring the bellums from the flooded area to the Euphrates and re-rafting them, the flotilla resumed the passage up-stream, and at 1700 hours anchored two miles south of Asani, at which hour gunfire was audible. This was an attempt of the Turks to shell our gun-boats at long range. At 2000 hours orders were received that the Battalion was to carry out a reconnaissance up the right bank starting early on July 7th. The night passed quietly, except for some heavy firing from a portion of the outpost line. At 0300 hours on July 7th the Battalion disembarked from the *Medjidieh* and moved up the right bank at 0345 hours. After advancing for about an hour the scouts reported that they had arrived at a creek some six feet deep and thirty yards broad, and as there were no cogent reasons for the whole Battalion to proceed half of " D " Company and the Battalion scouts were got across and the reconnaissance proceeded up as far as " Safety Point " at the Asani bend of the river. The remainder of the Battalion returned to the ship and re-embarked at 0615 hours.

Two hours later the Battalion was ordered ashore to embark on the *Muzafferi*. This steamer took the Battalion up-stream to " Safety Point," and here the Battalion disembarked and assembled under cover of the south side of Asani Village. Meanwhile the scouts and supporting half-company had established an observation line about one mile north of the village and some 1,700 yards from the Turkish main line of trenches on the right bank. The details on the observation line were relieved by 1100 hours, and the Battalion re-embarked on the *Muzafferi* and reached the *Medjidieh* at 1300 hours.

At 1515 hours orders were received to evacuate all stores from barges and ships and to pitch camp along the river bank. This was taken in hand at once and work continued until 1845 hours at which hour orders were received that the Battalion would embark on the *Muzafferi* at 2000 hours, land at " Safety Point," and thence make a night march to the observation line, where the Battalion, assisted by the 48th Pioneers, was to entrench the south bank of " Palm Grove Creek," actually the Umm as Sabiyan Creek. The line so entrenched was to be held as an advanced position and was known officially as " 24th Punjabis position." After a hasty meal the Battalion embarked on the *Muzafferi* and started up-stream, five bellums being taken in tow to transport ammunition, entrenching tools, etc. At 2115 hours the Battalion was clear of the *Muzafferi* and proceeded to the Palm Grove which marked the right of the line. By midnight the Battalion had assembled without mishap and at 0100 hours on July 8th work commenced. At 0430 hours work ceased and all movement was forbidden in view of possible artillery fire as soon as it became light.

At 0700 hours tentative orders were issued for the Battalion to move in bellums to attack the " Sandhills." Later this was changed, and the task of the capture of the Turkish piquet at Shukhair Village was allotted to the Regiment. Finally, however, operations were cancelled for forty-eight hours on account of the exhaustion of all troops consequent on over five days and nights of constant effort.

At 0900 hours the Turks showed much activity in extending their trenches and especially in demolishing the tops of towers in Shukhair village. From July 8th to 10th nothing of interest occurred except that the Turks and ourselves continued to improve our respective positions, while each evening officers reconnoitred towards the hostile trenches only to be pursued with ineffective long-range fire as soon as the return journey was commenced.

On the night of July 9th " Sixteen Palms " was occupied. This was a group of sixteen palms some 800 yards from the Turkish trenches. On the first night this was held with one double company and the Machine Gun Section. On the next night a Turkish patrol approached the piquet and was allowed to come up to a distance of thirty yards, when fire was opened with good results.

On the morning of July 11th the Turks introduced us to their guns, and at 0900 hours the first shell burst over the section of mountain artillery in our main position mortally wounding Major Blanford. They then switched on to Battalion Headquarters in the Palm Grove but fortunately did no damage. From the night of the 11th onwards the Turks became very nervy, a fact they demonstrated by ceaseless firing at night which developed at times into a heavy expenditure of shells, pom-pom shells, rockets, star shells and rifle ammunition. These displays were disturbing for a time. At intervals in the day-time also they swept our front with shell fire; generally, however, the range was over-estimated and bursts were too high. Still, it was evident that a gradual and marked improvement in their gunnery was taking place. On the night of July 12th Battalion Headquarters in the Palm Grove was treated to a general bombardment, which lasted from 2200 hours to midnight, and the Palm Grove had to be evacuated temporarily in consequence.

On July 13th the C.O. was called to Divisional Headquarters where orders were issued to move out in bellums and with two sections 30th Mountain Battery to attack the " Sandhills."

Action at the " Sandhills," Nasiriya, July 14th, 1915.

At 2030 hours on July 13th the Battalion was in readiness at the mouth of the Umm as Sabiyan Creek to take over the bellums sent up by the Division. At 2130 hours the bellums arrived; by 2300 hours the Battalion had embarked and had assembled in the marsh at the west exit of the creek. Here it was joined by two sections, 30th Mountain Battery. One sepoy was wounded during embarkation during which the Turks indulged in one of their most acute nervous attacks, bringing to bear every gun and rifle available.

At 0045 hours the advance due west commenced, the formation being single file. The pace was necessarily slow in order to keep pace with the slowest moving craft, which were those in which the mountain guns were embarked.

At about 0300 hours fire was opened on the column, evidently by a small piquet. The fire went high, and to the right. The column bore to the left so as to avoid the open water, and thenceforward progress through the reeds was very slow and exhausting, as it was necessary to man-handle the bellums continually. The hostile fire persisted and followed the column for some distance; it then ceased. About 0345 hours heavy fire was opened on the column from the north-east—the bullets were again high and well to the rear. The two sections of guns with "B" Company as escort were now detached to the south-west, where they were instructed to wait until dawn.

The remainder of the Battalion then pushed north-west until 0430 hours when patches of marshland were reached. It was decided to halt until there was sufficient light to fix the Battalion's position. At about 0500 hours it was possible to make out that the Battalion was 1,700 yards due west of the Sandhills, and therefore in rear of them. Lieut.-Colonel Climo decided to move east in bellums up to 1,000 yards from the objective, and after a short bombardment by the guns to attack the rear of the position. His reasons for the plan were that he wished to obtain a decision before the Turks could be reinforced and before the Arabs to the west or north-west could collect to intervene.

By the time the Battalion had disembarked from the bellums the mountain guns and machine guns were in position, the former at the point where they found themselves at daybreak, about 1,300 yards south-west, and the latter about 900 yards west of the objective. Fire effect was obtained at once and in a very few minutes the position appeared to be covered with dust and smoke.

The advance commenced at 0515 hours and was carried out with dash and rapidity to about 200 yards from the position. During the advance the men had to wade in water which varied from eighteen inches to four feet in depth, the bottom being composed of mud and pitted with holes one to two feet deep. At intervals open creeks were crossed which were subjected to heavy fire as the companies crossed them.

Before the last reserve company left the bellums occasional shots from the rear indicated that the local Arabs were inclined to give trouble. Lieut.-Colonel Climo left the bellum escort to the battery to deal with this and made his way forward to a distance of about 250 yards from the position. The aspect of affairs was promising, and a survey of the situation pointed to the advisability of assaulting the right flank of the Sandhills. He therefore returned to hurry forward the two reserve companies and to send up a fresh supply of ammunition.

Just before he left the firing line No. 4 Double Company, the first to go into action, rose to the assault, but after going a few yards recoiled under a storm of fire to the point they had started from.

On his way back, Lieut.-Colonel Climo met one reserve company which was sent to the left of the line. He then proceeded to the bellums, about 600 yards from the firing line, where he ascertained that the other reserve company had been drawn into a fight with the Arabs in the neighbourhood of the guns.

Lieut.-Colonel Climo now collected five or six bellums and, while doing so, perceived that a general withdrawal from the firing line was in progress. This was at about 0700 hours. It was ascertained later that the order to retire was issued by a British officer owing to the risk of running out of ammunition and the increasing danger from the Arab attack in rear and on the flank.

As it was desirable to ascertain whether any companies were still hanging on near the hostile position, Major Dent (staff), Lieutenant Birkbeck, Lieutenant Pim and Lieut.-Colonel Climo, accompanied by twenty to thirty men, returned towards the position with five bellums. It was hoped that with the extra ammunition and this small reinforcement, the position might yet be captured from the Turks, who had been retiring in twos and threes since 0600 hours. The small reinforcing party arrived at a point about 300 yards from the Sandhills, where a party of the Battalion was found waiting for ammunition. Here fire was opened on the enemy, but in a few moments a good proportion of the party was killed or wounded. A new element was now introduced into the situation by the opening of fire by three Turkish guns from the left flank. This fire swept that portion of the marsh over which the attack had taken place. Lieut.-Colonel Climo now decided that it was advisable to withdraw, as every moment of delay would add to the difficulty of getting the mountain guns and machine guns to a place of safety.

It was with great reluctance that he decided to abandon further search for stragglers and officers. The bellums were pushed back with the killed and wounded towards the guns, and in the meantime the Arabs had come in so close that the party had to run the gauntlet under fire at forty yards from either side. Fortunately both machine guns were in working order, and their fire enabled the party to reach open water and safety. Eventually the mountain guns were reached; their fire had covered the withdrawal with great effect, notwithstanding that they in turn were being subjected to Arab fire from the rear and from both flanks.

Here was picked up "B" Company (the battery escort), and the greater part of "A" and "C" Companies. The latter company, one of the reserve, had been unable to move forward to reinforce owing to the determined endeavour on the part of the Arabs to seize the entire fleet of the bellums. "C" Company had frustrated this manœuvre and had then removed the majority of the bellums to the vicinity of the mountain guns.

Lieut.-Colonel Climo now reorganized the remnants of the force for the final retirement. The bellums were divided into three portions, two to escort the sections of guns, the third portion with the machine guns as rear-guard. The withdrawal commenced at 0805 hours. The Turks had advanced a portion of their force from the Sandhills and were maintaining a considerable volume of fire on the mountain guns and bellums at a range of 700 yards, while at the same time the Arabs to the north-west were endeavouring to hamper the withdrawal. To this was added the fire of the majority of the Turkish guns, the range and direction being unusually accurate. All these attentions were intensified as soon as it was apparent that a withdrawal was in progress. The mountain guns coming into action by alternate sections kept down the fire from the Turks, while the bellum escort dealt with the Arab fire. The rear-guard, meanwhile, acted against the Arabs following up from the north. Unfortunately one machine gun was disabled, but the fire of the other was very effective throughout.

The withdrawal was necessarily very slow owing to the continual grounding of the gun rafts and bellums in the shallows. For the first hour shell and rifle fire were incessant, and many shells burst within a few feet of the fleet without effecting more than a few casualties, and during the next hour of the withdrawal the enemy's fire increased in intensity and accuracy. At 1000 hours the force arrived under cover of the "24th Punjabis's position," and from then onwards the strain on the troops ceased to exist.

The withdrawal was carried out under distinctly critical conditions: that it was not closely pursued by the Turks may be ascribed to the severe handling experienced by the garrison of the Sandhills and to the accurate fire of the mountain guns, machine guns, and rifles of the escorts.

To return to the attack, it appears evident that the garrison of the Sandhills had been reinforced just previous to our advance, for grouped round the north end of the position were fifteen to twenty empty bellums. In the advance up to 250 yards from the objective very few casualties were sustained. At this point the treachery of the Arabs began to make itself felt, and the two leading companies were subjected to heavy close-range fire which occasioned such serious casualties that in a very short space of time six out of eight British officers were killed, and the major portion of these two companies were put out of action. It is evident that had the offensive been persisted in the battalion would have been annihilated.

The casualties in this action were:—

Killed.—6 British officers and 50 Indian other ranks.
Wounded.—3 Indian officers and 88 Indian other ranks.

This represents over 33 per cent. of the numbers engaged. The British officers killed in this engagement were Major H. W. F. Cooke, Major S. Morton, Captain E. H. le M. Sinkinson, Captain G. Leslie-Smith, Lieutenant M. Birkbeck and Lieutenant Haverfield, I.A.R.O.

Great efforts were made to carry back the dead, but in many cases this was frustrated by the Arabs. The high proportion of killed to wounded is to be ascribed to the depth of water in which so many were shot down. A number of officers and men were originally reported to be missing. In no single case, however, was a missing man subsequently reported to be a prisoner. There is no doubt, therefore, that the missing were either killed outright or, having been seriously wounded, fell in the marsh and were drowned. This was borne out by the result of a subsequent visit to the battlefield in September, after the floods had subsided. The skeletons of all the British officers were identified and numbers of those of the Indian other ranks were discovered. As many were buried as time permitted.

Although the attack was a failure it was nevertheless a gallant failure. Much sympathy was extended to the Battalion, as it was realized that the enterprise was an impossible one in the circumstances. The garrison had been reinforced and the attempt amounted to an attack over deep water against strong opposition and with insufficient fire support. It was an attempt to react " Townshend's Regatta " at Qurna on a smaller scale, but with the difference that the fire support was less and the flanks of the attack exposed. It was, however, a matter for congratulation that troops who had been subjected to such a severe handling had extricated themselves successfully from a situation in which they found themselves surrounded.

As the official history of the war states: " It was only the cool skill of their Commander, the steadfastness of the officers and men of the 24th, and the steady and valuable covering fire of the 30th Mountain Battery Guns and their escort that finally effected the desired concentration near the guns."

In addition to awards to the Indian ranks, Lieutenant H. M. Pim and Captain R. C. Clifford, Indian Medical Service, were awarded the Military Cross.

The day of July 15th was quiet, the Battalion finding a piquet of 200 rifles and one machine gun at Shukhair, but the night of July 15th-16th was disturbed, as the Turks were jumpy and kept up continuous sniping and bursts of fire. This happened for several days, until the 22nd; the day as a rule being quiet while there was sniping at night. On July 23rd operation orders for the battle of Nasiriya were issued. The general plan was that the 12th Infantry Brigade operating on the left bank was to attack at 0530 hours, covering fire being given by the troops on the right bank. At 0600 hours the 30th Infantry Brigade, after a bombardment, was to attack on the right bank, cross the Majinina Creek and capture the Turkish position to the north of the creek.

In accordance with these orders the 24th Punjabis was detailed to take over Sixteen Palms piquet, Shukhair Village, and the trenches between them. This line was taken over at 2130 hours on July 23rd; head cover was made with sandbags and the trenches improved. The night was much disturbed by Turkish sniping and frequent outbursts of fire.

At 0530 hours the 24th Punjabis and the machine guns of the 30th Brigade opened fire from our line on the trenches in front of Thorneycroft Point, in support of the attack on the left bank.

At 0550 hours the Turkish guns opened on Shukhair Village. Fortunately their fire was directed on the village itself, thus missing the massed machine guns sited close to and to the east of it. About seven to eight guns and two pom-poms were thus engaged, but the liberal use of sandbags for head cover, made during the previous night, minimized casualties.

The attack on the left bank slowed up at 0615 hours, and at 0630 hours the 30th Brigade began its advance, covered chiefly by machine-gun fire which switched to the left as the Brigade advanced.

At about 0845 hours the troops detailed for the assault were approaching the Majinina Creek, and about 0900 hours the eastern half of the Turkish position on the right bank was assaulted. The fire of the Battalion and the machine guns was then turned on to the Turks retiring from their right flank. Fire ceased at 0930 hours.

At 1100 hours the Battalion moved to the " Old Well " in the Turkish position and remained in brigade reserve for the rest of the day. The Battalion bivouacked with the remainder of the Brigade about $1\frac{1}{2}$ miles north of the Majinina position, with the 12th Infantry Brigade on the opposite bank of the river. On the next day the Battalion marched in brigade to a bivouac opposite Nasiriya on the right bank of the Euphrates.

Only slight casualties were suffered on July 24th, amounting to one killed and eleven Indian other ranks wounded.

The Turkish artillery were sometimes accurate with their first shell, even though their fire might generally be ineffective. So it was on this day, as the following incident shows :—

The Commanding Officer, an Afridi Havildar and Bugler were looking over the breastwork covering the Shukhair Village watching the progress of the battle on the left bank. The C.O. remarked casually to the two Afridis : " It is strange that the Turks have not opened artillery fire yet. Is it possible that they have withdrawn their guns preparatory to a general retirement ?" At that moment a spurt of dust was seen about 2,000 yards behind the Turkish front-line trenches. This was the first Turkish shell. It burst on impact twenty yards in front of the three observers. The bugler was killed with two shrapnel bullets in the head, the havildar was hit in the shoulder, and the C.O. received a considerable portion of the parapet in his chest. Thus the first shell fired at Shukhair Village on the morning of July 24th was successful, just as the first shell fired on July 11th mortally wounded Major Blanford, R.A. Strangely enough on both these days no further casualties were suffered from the Turkish artillery, though this was not due to lack of endeavour on their part.

The following Orders of the Day were issued:—

From His Majesty the King Emperor: "The splendid achievement of General Gorringe's column in spite of many hardships and intense heat fills me with admiration. Please convey my heartiest congratulation to all ranks who took part in these successful operations."

From the Army Commander: "I cannot say too much to you and your splendid troops for the magnificent success you have achieved. The confidence I have always in the 12th Division has been amply fulfilled."

From Major-General Melliss, the Brigade Commander, from the Divisional Commander, H.E. the Viceroy and General Sir Ian Hamilton congratulations were received for the way all had endured hardship, heat and privations, and on the success achieved.

The Turkish forces during these operations amounted to about 4,200, with 15 guns; and in addition there were large numbers of Arabs. The Turks throughout had fought stubbornly, and their losses were calculated to have been 2,000. Five hundred Turkish dead were counted after the battle of July 24th. All fifteen guns were captured, and in addition nearly 1,000 prisoners. In other words the Turkish force in the Nasiriya area practically ceased to exist.

The congratulatory telegrams quoted above were well earned, for in addition to the stubborn resistance put up by the Turks the climatic conditions under which the troops worked could hardly have been worse. The troops were engaged for twenty days without cessation at a time when it was quite common to have a shade temperature of 113° F. with a damp and humid atmosphere.

As General Nixon wrote in his despatch: "Seldom, if ever, have our troops been called upon to campaign in more trying heat than they have experienced this summer in the marshy plains of Mesopotamia. Many indeed succumbed to the effects of the sun, when trenches had to be manned without a vestige of shade; and others were worn out by illness and by restless nights spent in digging and carrying stores from the ships, or disturbed by the attacks or fire of the enemy."

It is unfortunate that these operations have not been commemorated by the grant of a battle honour Nasiriya. Apart from the material results attained under the worst climatic conditions the British force, between July 5th and 24th, suffered 944 battle casualties.

On July 26th the Battalion was ordered to be ready for duty on the lines of communication in the vicinity of the Akaika Channel. It remained in bivouac until July 31st, with a reconnaissance by half the Battalion on the 30th as the only incident.

From August 1st to September 8th the chief event was the arrival of reinforcements of officers. The following joined: Lieut.-Colonel Cummins; Captain Trevor; Captain Sutherland, 22nd Punjabis; Captain

C. A. Bignell, 4th Rajputs; Captain Black, 11th Rajputs, and Second-Lieutenants Hockey and H. Browne, I.A.R.O.

Lieut.-Colonel Cummins took over command from Lieut.-Colonel Climo on August 19th, on the latter's succeeding temporarily to the command of the 30th Infantry Brigade.

On September 8th the outposts on the right bank of the Euphrates were handed over to the 90th Punjabis, and the Regiment embarked on the "T.1" for Amara. Leaving Nasiriya at 0400 hours the Battalion reached the Akaika Dam at noon on September 8th, where No. 4 Double Company under Captain Sutherland rejoined the Battalion; and Kubaish was reached on the 9th at 0830 hours, where No. 1 Double Company was picked up. The Battalion arrived at Qurna at noon on September 10th, and embarked on the "P.5" for Amara the same day. On reaching Amara on the morning of the 14th the Battalion disembarked and went into billets on the right bank of the Chahela Creek.

The Battalion remained at Amara until September 21st, when Nos. 1 and 2 Double Companies, under Captain Bignell, left with the 30th Brigade Headquarters for Ali Gharbi.

A draft of 54 Indian other ranks arrived from the depot on September 28th. From this date up to October 23rd nothing of importance occurred so far as the Battalion was concerned. Lieut.-Colonel Climo rejoined on October 16th, after commanding two battalions of the 30th Infantry Brigade which were engaged in the first battle of Kut-el-Amara (September 27th and 28th).

Prior to the first battle of Kut-el-Amara a Motor Machine Gun Section was formed for use as divisional troops. The guns were carried in improvised armoured cars, from which fire could be delivered on the move. The machine gunner personnel was found entirely from the 24th, and the section was under command of Captain Trevor. This section took part in the first battle of Kut-el-Amara, attached to General Delamain's column. In the battle of Ctesiphon the section was attached to the "Flying Column" under General Melliss, with which it worked during the first two days of the battle. When the force arrived back at Aziziya, during the retreat to Kut, the section was broken up and the personnel rejoined the Battalion.

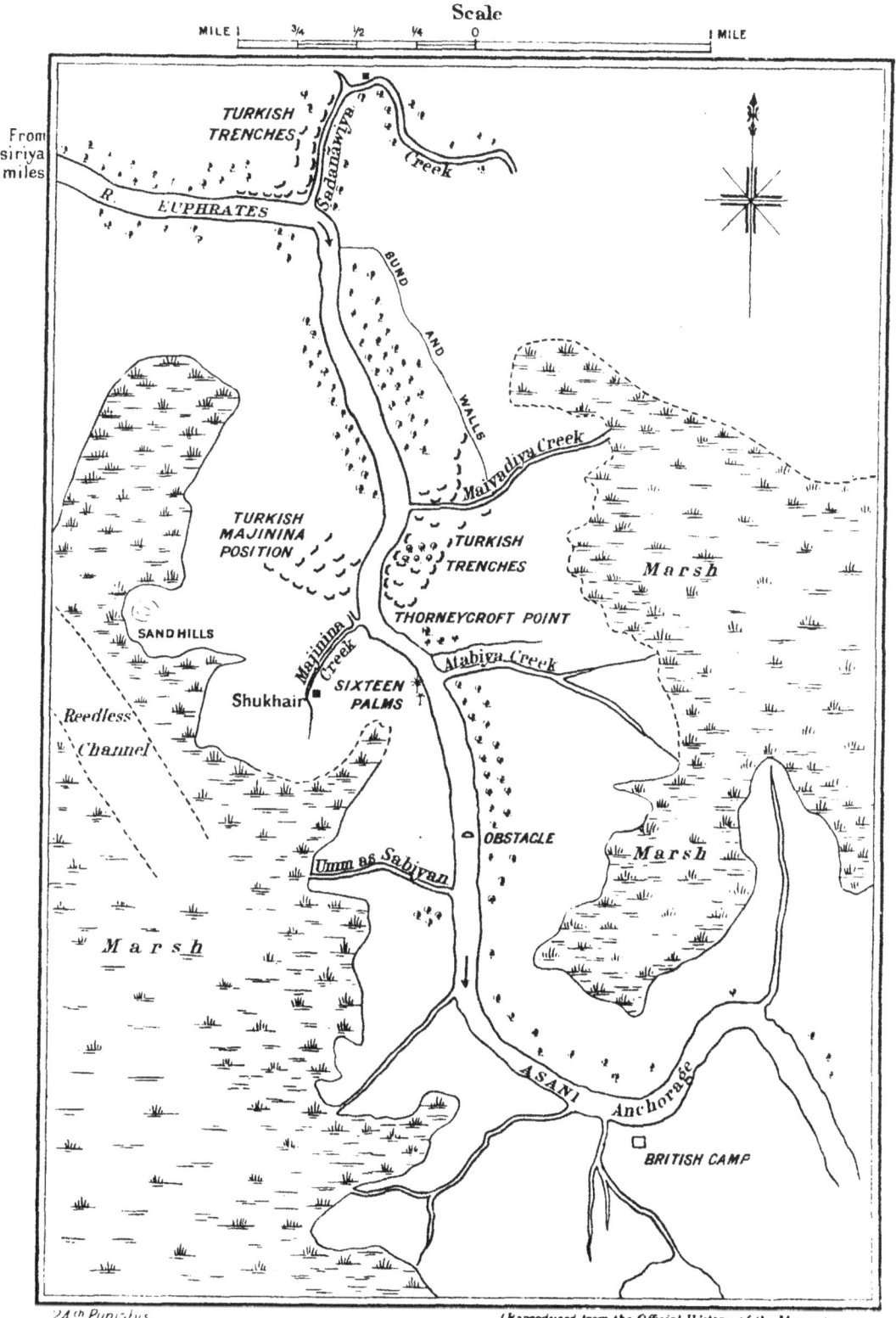

CHAPTER IV.

THE BATTLE OF CTESIPHON AND RETREAT TO KUT.

FOR the period covered by this and the succeeding chapter there are practically no records. The war diaries of the Battalion up to and including the battle of Ctesiphon were lost in the Tigris, owing to the sinking of the barge, on which they were loaded, during the retreat to Kut on December 1st, 1915, the day of the engagement at Umm-ul-Tubul. The war diaries for the period of the siege of Kut were destroyed by order on the fall of that place, and no copy (perhaps foolishly, though according to orders) was kept. The only Battalion records available consist of a report of the operations of the 30th Composite Infantry Brigade by Colonel Climo, a brief account by Lieut.-Colonel Cummins of the first attack at Ctesiphon, and a report of the second day's fighting at Ctesiphon by Captain Haig, who, by that time, was the only British officer left with the half-battalion engaged. Hence the story of the Battalion's history during this period has had to be written up some time after the event, and partly from memory.

During October, 1915, the units of the 6th Division and of the 30th Infantry Brigade were brought up to establishment. The Battalion was eventually completed with a draft of 100 other ranks from the 123rd Outram's Rifles under command of Lieutenant Stapleton, I.A.R.O. The men of this draft, with the exception of a few N.C.Os., were recruits of eight months' service. Other battalions in the Force at this time received similar drafts. It was our first experience of the receipt in any numbers of what we considered partially trained men, and we considered ourselves badly treated in consequence. However, the best had to be made of this material in the short time available for training. By the last week in October the Battalion was up to strength.

On the 24th of the month the Battalion started on its march to Kut, escorting a mahela convoy. The detachment at Ali Gharbi was picked up on October 30th and this made the Battalion complete. The task of escorting a mahela convoy caused the marches to be of uneven length, as the distance marched usually depended on the wind and the bends of the river; and upon the two latter depended the distance that the mahelas could sail in a day. On November 8th, however, Kut was reached. The battlefield of Es Sinn was passed, and farther down the river the Wadi and the area between Hanna and Sunnaiyat, the scene a few months later of some of the most sanguinary and heartbreaking reverses sustained by the Tigris Corps in their gallant efforts to relieve the beleaguered garrison of Kut. In this latter area in November, 1915, all was peaceful and the ground untouched by pick and shovel. No sign was seen of the large

Suwaikiyeh marsh, of evil memory for the Tigris Corps in the spring of 1916.

On arrival in Kut it was found that the troops destined for the attempt on Baghdad were being pushed up to Aziziya as fast as possible by small echelons. The Battalion marched again on November 11th, reaching Aziziya, after three long marches, on November 13th.

The officers now present with the Battalion were:—

Brevet Colonel S. H. Climo, D.S.O., Commanding.
Lieut.-Colonel H. A. V. Cummins, Second-in-Command.
Captain A. O. Sutherland, 22nd Punjabis attached.
Captain A. B. Haig, Adjutant.
Captain C. A. Bignell, 4th Rajputs attached.
Lieutenant H. C. Dillon, 26th Punjabis attached.
Lieutenant E. S. Rind, Quartermaster.
Lieutenant H. C. Stapleton, I.A.R.O.
Lieutenant E. L. Duxbury, I.A.R.O.
Lieutenant W. W. A. Phillips, I.A.R.O.
Lieutenant H. Browne, I.A.R.O.
Captain R. C. Clifford, M.C., I.M.S., Medical Officer.
Captain A. C. H. Trevor was in charge of the Motor Machine Gun Section.

Lieutenant C. H. K. Phillips, I.A.R.O., had just left on appointment as A.D.C. to General Gorringe.

As regards Indian officers there were many changes from those who had originally left with the Battalion on service in October, 1914. Some had been killed, more had been wounded, and others were sick. Among the more notable casualties had been Subedars Gul Akbar ("C" Company) and Sahib Nur ("F" Company), the former wounded and the latter killed. Subedar-Major Sakt Chand, Subedars Labh Singh, Ali Muhammad and Jemadar Amir Khan had all been wounded and were in India.

Diwan Singh was now Subedar Major, and the other Indian officers present were:—

"A" Company.—Subedar Hashim Ali and Jemadar Ghulam Mahomed.
"B" Company.—Subedar Kishan Singh and Jemadar Fateh Singh.
"C" Company.—Jemadar Lal Mir and Jemadar Sher Nur.
"D" Company.—Subedar Jhanda Singh.
"E" Company.—Jemadar Pirthi Chand.
"F" Company.—Subedar Umar Khan.
"G" Company.—Subedar-Major Diwan Singh, Jemadar Ujagar Singh and Jemadar Bhola Singh.
"H" Company.—Subedar Sawan Singh and Jemadar Narain Singh.
Jemadar Sohan Singh, M.C., was Indian Adjutant.

On arrival at Aziziya it was discovered that the intention was to leave the Battalion behind as the post garrison. This was due to the fact that the Battalion included Afridis. It was only owing to the force of character and personality of Colonel Climo, who interviewed General Townshend, the Force Commander, that the orders were changed. When, therefore, the 6th Division and 30th Brigade finally left Aziziya on their desperate venture, Headquarters and Nos. 1 and 3 Double Companies formed part of the force. The remainder were left as the post garrison of Aziziya under command of Captain A. O. Sutherland. The Sikh companies of Nos. 1 and 3 Double Companies were made up to strength from those of Nos. 2 and 4 Double Companies. Consequently the detachment left behind consisted of the Afridis, the 100-strong draft of the 123rd Outram's Rifles, and a comparatively small number of Sikhs.

Headquarters and the half-battalion engaged in the battle numbered seven British officers (including the Medical Officer and Captain Trevor, who was detached in command of the Motor Machine Gun Section), nine Indian officers, and 326 Indian other ranks. It may safely be stated that this half-battalion was second to none among the Indian troops. They were fit, well trained, and imbued with the highest morale.

It is only fair to state that the Afridi specialists (machine gunners, signallers, etc.) were bitterly disappointed at not being allowed to proceed with the Battalion. Actually, up to the end of April, 1916, the Battalion lost seven men (Afridis) by desertion; five at Nasiriya, two during the siege of Kut, while two more attempted to desert during the siege but their courage failed them and they returned. This, taken in all, was not a bad result, since cases in other battalions occurred of Punjabi Mohammedans and even of Hindus deserting to the Mussalman enemy. But this result was only obtained by the exercise of unremitting care and unceasing precautions.

As already stated, the Battalion arrived at Aziziya on November 13th, 1915. Here the whole force destined for the attack on Baghdad was concentrated. Here also a halt was made for some days, while the last arrangements as regards supplies, etc., were made, and the necessary reserves of all war-like stores collected. On November 17th the march towards Ctesiphon began. Only a short march was made on this day to El Kutenie. The Battalion started late in the day, having been detailed as escort to the second line transport of the whole force. This transport was composed of a heterogeneous collection of camels, mules, donkeys and bullocks. On arrival at El Kutenie there was an alarm that the Turks were advancing, and trenches were dug. The alarm, however, proved to be groundless. On the 18th the advance was continued to Zor, where a small Turkish force was reported. After a brief skirmish the enemy retired. On the 19th the main force marched to Lajj, while Colonel Climo, with the 24th and 76th Punjabis and a battery, was sent to follow the course of the river and to guard the ship convoy round some awkward bends in the river. No opposition was met with and the Arab villages were all flying the white flag, and pretended friendliness. This small force bivouacked for the night of the 19th-20th some miles short of Lajj, to which place the force marched the next morning.

The officers now present with the Headquarters and the half-battalion which were to take part in the ensuing battle were:—

Brevet Colonel S. H. Climo, D.S.O.
Lieut.-Colonel H. A. V. Cummins.
Captain A. B. Haig.
Lieutenant H. C. Dillon.
Lieutenant E. S. Rind.
Captain R. C. Clifford, M.C., I.M.S.

The remainder were at Aziziya, while Captain Bignell was on the sick list.

At Lajj the 30th Infantry Brigade (24th and 76th Punjabis, and 2nd/7th Gurkha Rifles) was temporarily broken up. General Melliss was given command of what was called the flying column. This included the 6th Cavalry Brigade and the 76th Punjabis in A.T. Carts. A composite 30th Infantry Brigade was formed, commanded by Colonel Climo, with Captain Haig as his staff officer. This Brigade consisted of the 24th Punjabis and 2nd/7th Gurkha Rifles, with the addition of the 66th Punjabis and 117th Mahrattas from the 16th Brigade.

The Turkish position at Ctesiphon (a position which had been under construction for some months) consisted on the left bank of about six miles of trenches with redoubts every four to five hundred yards. Only three miles of this line was open to attack, as the other three miles ran into a loop of the river. The three miles farthest from the river ran from the vicinity of what was termed High Wall to V.P. (or Vital Point). Between these two points was a redoubt, called by us Water or Delamain Redoubt. The left of the Turkish line at Vital Point consisted of a very strong redoubt, wired and prepared for all-round defence. The redoubt was constructed round two small mounds some twenty to thirty feet above the level of the surrounding country and so offering a good landmark in the flat and featureless plains of Mesopotamia. Behind the Turkish first line and behind High Wall was the famous Arch of Ctesiphon. This was the ruins of a palace of the Khusroes, and a remarkable relic of the past. Near this arch was a small mound, subsequently named Gurkha Mound, and on which the 24th Punjabis fought gallantly on the second day of the battle. Four hundred yards north of the arch was the village and tomb of Suliman Pak. This man was reputed to be the Prophet's barber, and his tomb was held in veneration by Mohammedans. The Turkish name for the battle is Suliman Pak, taken from the name of the village.

Farther in rear the Turks had a second line which was incomplete and unwired and which we never reached. The first line was wired throughout; the wire was complete from High Wall to Vital Point but was not so good in the portion of the line contained in the river loop. The wire consisted of a high single fence. This, although not up to the standard of wire on other fronts during the war, was good and effective against our small quantity of artillery, which was not provided with any high explosive.

The general plan of the battle was that the force, numbering some 14,000 of all ranks, was divided into four columns (" A," " B," " C " and Flying). " C " was nearest the river and was to make the initial attack; " B " was on the outer flank and was to make the next attack coming in on the flank of the Turkish first line. " A," which was intended for the main attack, was to assault Vital Point when the other two attacks had been launched. The Flying Column was to move on the Turkish second line and pursue to Baghdad. Column " A," under command of Major-General Delamain consisted of the 30th composite Infantry Brigade (composition given above) plus the 2nd Dorsets and 104th Rifles, which two Battalions were retained as a reserve in General Delamain's own hands.

On the afternoon of November 21st Column " C " started its march, openly and ostentatiously, keeping near the river, with the idea of making the Turks believe that the chief attack was to come near the river. Soon after dark the remainder of the force started off in two long and parallel columns. The track led for some distance between the ruined banks of the ancient Nahrwan Canal. The night march was accomplished without incident and Column " A " got to its appointed position some three miles from Vital Point at 0015 hours on November 22nd. Here the columns parted Company, " B " and Flying Columns proceeding farther on to their allotted rendezvous.

On arrival in position Lieutenant Rind, with the scouts of the 24th Punjabis and 2nd/7th Gurkha Rifles was sent out to try and discover a water-course marked on the air sketch map, which was used for the battle. After an absence of two hours he returned and reported that this water-course was non-existent. He was proved right in the morning, when it was seen that what had been mistaken for a water-course from the air was in reality a well defined path in the grass. This patrol had moved close up to a Turkish piquet without being observed, had seen reliefs taking place and had made out a mound in rear, which was thought to be Vital Point. Meanwhile Column " A " proceeded to dig in on the bank of the canal. This work was finished about 0500 hours and the men got a little rest until daylight. The night was very cold. On leaving Lajj the men carried cooked rations for the 22nd and 23rd. For water there was only available the men's water-bottles and the company pakhals. No more water was likely to be available until the Tigris or Diyala was reached. Soon after dawn a Turkish patrol galloped up towards the line of the

Nahrwan Canal. No firing was permitted, and the patrol returned. At daylight it was possible to see the two mounds of Vital Point clearly visible in the morning light, and the Arch of Ctesiphon away to the left front stood out as an imposing landmark. About 0800 hours Colonel Climo issued his final orders for the attack. This was to be carried out by the 24th Punjabis on the right and the 2nd/7th Gurkha Rifles on the left, on a frontage respectively of 300 and 600 yards. The 66th Punjabis and 117th Mahrattas were to follow in support.

It was impressed on the men that the attack was to be carried out rapidly, reliance being placed on artillery and machine-gun fire up till the moment of assault. As will be seen from the subsequent narrative the men carried out their part to the letter. At 0900 hours the advance began in lines of platoons in fours. The artillery support available was ten guns—six 18-pounders and four old howitzers of 5 in. calibre. The advance continued in complete silence until it was thought that the Turks might have withdrawn, so long was their fire withheld. At length after an advance of 3,000 yards, and when the leading troops were only 1,000 yards from the trenches, a hail of musketry and artillery fire opened. Without hesitating or waiting to fire the two leading battalions rushed on, and in twenty minutes the position was captured. This was a magnificent performance. Our artillery support was negligible; the wire was uncut, and the field of fire for the Turks was perfect. But the position was captured at the cost of very heavy casualties. The half-battalion must have lost nearly 60 per cent. of its strength in these few minutes. Lieut.-Colonel Cummins was wounded and Lieutenant Rind killed, while Lieutenant Dillon was hit in the shoulder whilst lying against the wire, endeavouring to cut it with his wire-cutters. Incidentally no wire-cutters were issued, and the only ones in the Battalion were private ones owned by individual officers.

Many were the deeds of gallantry performed here. Many were unrecorded in detail as the observers were themselves subsequently killed. Men were seen standing against the wire and holding the strands apart for others to crawl through. It is on record that 4375 Havildar Sundar Singh, a noted athlete and long jumper, took a running jump clean over the wire and dashed on to be killed in the Turkish trenches fifty yards farther on. When once the Turkish trenches were reached there was a considerable amount of bayonet work, and the trenches were in many cases choked with the bodies of Turks, Punjabis and Gurkhas.

The Turks were now seen to be retreating in large numbers, and fire with good effect was opened on them at ranges varying from 200 yards upwards. As soon as the retreating Turks were beyond effective range the task of rallying the Brigade was begun. This was not easy owing to the intermixture of units, the heavy casualties, and the necessity of rounding up and guarding the eight or nine hundred prisoners captured, and also to the intricacy of the trenches.

Before finishing the account of this first attack it will be as well to put on record the remarks of Colonel Climo (the temporary Brigade Commander and permanent Commanding Officer of the Battalion):—

" I hope I may be permitted to place on record my impressions of the 30th Composite Brigade hastily formed the previous day, and composed entirely of Indian troops. They were given a formidable task and were proud of it. Throughout the first attack there was not a moment's hesitation, not an individual case of men falling out to attend to wounded, and not a sign of irresolution among the lines as they passed over the field strewn with killed and wounded. I cannot resist expressing my admiration and heartfelt gratitude to the Composite Brigade on their indomitable fortitude and their devotion to duty and their indifference to danger, qualities which enabled them to push home their attack in marvellously short time from start to finish and to oust a force of Turks which, at the moment of assault, must have out-numbered the remnants of the Brigade by four to one. Out of the indiscriminate pack of units which broke its way through the barbed wire, the honour of reaching the enemy's trenches first lies with an intermixture of the 24th and 66th Punjabis. A captured officer of the 3rd Anatolian Regiment remarked that he was astounded at the bravery and determination of the Indian troops and that he could not have believed it possible for such a position to be carried in the manner and space of time it was."

The brigaded machine guns operated on the right of the Brigade. The Brigade Machine Gun Officer reported that the guns of the 24th Punjabis were worked excellently and, having due regard to the very heavy casualties incurred early in the action, that it was highly creditable that the guns were brought into action in the forward position.

After reorganization had been completed the Brigade was ordered to advance and capture eight Turkish guns some 1,800 yards farther on which had apparently been abandoned by the enemy. The guns at any rate were not being served. The Brigade carried out this advance, reinforced by half a battalion of the 2nd Dorsets. The 24th Punjabis were in support during this advance and were now under the command of Lieutenant H. C. Dillon, who, although wounded in the shoulder, continued to fight. He was the only British officer now left with the Battalion.

The Turks made strenuous efforts to prevent the capture of these guns, and their shell fire was particularly heavy and accurate. They were bursting their shrapnel remarkably low, contrary to what we had often experienced before. The Brigade, however, was not to be denied and the guns were captured, but the attackers were brought to a standstill after advancing a short distance past the guns. This was at about 1130 hours. At 1150 hours a message was received from the Brigade Major of Column " A " directing half a battalion to be sent back to Vital Point. The 24th Punjabis were accordingly sent back under Lieutenant Dillon. On arrival at Vital

Point the Battalion, with some of the Dorsets and other details of Column "A" was directed to advance along the Turkish first line towards the Water Redoubt, which was still held by the Turks, and against which the 17th Brigade (Column "C") could make no headway. The advance took place, the Battalion being on the right of the Dorsets. The line advanced by short rushes up to about 150 yards of the enemy's work, when, reinforced by the 22nd Company S. & M., and in conjunction with the attack of the 17th Brigade the redoubt was captured. Lieutenant Dillon was once more wounded when cutting the wire, this time through the stomach. It was a mortal wound and he died, to everyone's regret, during the course of the night. His action during the whole day had been most gallant and he set a fine example to all ranks.

After the capture of Water Redoubt the remains of the Battalion advanced to a line in front of the Ctesiphon Arch. At this stage the battle was stabilizing along the whole front, and the Battalion, now without any British officers was ordered back to Vital Point by Brigadier-General Hoghton of the 17th Brigade. The Battalion arrived at Vital Point about 1700 hours. Eventually orders were received for the remains of the Battalion to act as a guard for the night to a Field Ambulance situated between Vital Point and the Water Redoubt, and here it spent the night.

The action of the Battalion Machine Gun Section during the remainder of the first day of the battle must now be recorded. As already mentioned the guns were very well handled under the direct command of the senior N.C.O., 4489 Naik Sundar, "E" Company, and were with, or even slightly in advance of the general line of the firing line of the Brigade during the onward advance from Vital Point.

When the Battalion was ordered back to Vital Point the Machine Gun Section did not accompany it. Consequently when the Brigade was finally brought to a halt, after the capture of the Turkish guns already referred to, the machine guns were in a very exposed position. Captain Haig was sent by Colonel Climo to withdraw them a short distance. The section had already suffered severely, and so depleted was one gun's crew that Captain Haig had to carry back the gun itself into its new position. When this officer arrived back at Colonel Climo's position he found that the latter had been wounded for the second time through the leg. While being assisted back to a stretcher Colonel Climo was again wounded, this being the third time during the day. He appeared to attract bullets on this morning, for his orderly, Lance-Naik Kishan Singh, was hit through the top of the thigh when actually carrying one end of the stretcher.

After the departure of Colonel Climo the Turks developed a strong counter-attack. This had the result of forcing back the very weak line of the 30th Composite Brigade some distance towards Vital Point and in the loss of the eight guns previously captured. During this counter-attack the remainder of the team of one machine gun became casualties and the gun was accordingly lost. The other gun was only brought out of action by the gallantry of 514 Lance-Naik Pal Singh, assisted by a man of the Dorsets. Pal Singh was awarded the I.O.M. but was subsequently killed during the siege of Kut. This gun had been temporarily rendered useless as the tangent sight had been shot away. On Colonel Climo becoming a casualty the 30th Composite Brigade ceased to exist, and the units came under the direct command of General Delamain, of Column " A." Captain Haig accordingly endeavoured to find the remnants of the 24th Punjabis. After advancing again from Vital Point with stragglers of various units he eventually found himself with the 18th Brigade of Column " B," and returned with them about midnight to Vital Point. No sign of the Battalion was to be found here, but in the morning, November 23rd, after collecting what was left of the Machine Gun Section, he found the remnants of the Battalion in the position already described between Vital Point and the Water Redoubt. Only about 100 rifles remained. These were marched to the Water Redoubt, where General Delamain now had his headquarters. On arrival orders were received to proceed to the mound by the arch of Ctesiphon, where the 2nd/7th Gurkhas already were.

This mound was subsequently named Gurkha Mound. The detachment, which consisted of 400 rifles of the 2nd/7th Gurkhas and 110 rifles of the 24th Punjabis with the addition of the maxim-gun battery, had been placed on this mound to prevent the Turks getting between the river and Water Redoubt and so in the rear of the British force. The mound was some twenty to thirty feet high and within 100 yards of the arch. Some 400 yards away to the north was the village and tomb of Suliman Pak. The 24th Punjabis held that portion of the mound nearest the arch, and also dug a trench to face the open ground between the arch and Suliman Pak.

For some two hours before dark the mound was steadily bombarded by the Turkish artillery, who were endeavouring to locate two of our field guns in position near the arch. It was remarkable how the Turks managed to avoid hitting the arch. Their shrapnel was mainly burst high, and what bullets fell on the Battalion were mostly spent. About 1730 hours there were signs of an advance on the part of the Turks, and sniping fire commenced, culminating at times in bursts of heavy fire. This continued throughout the night and only ceased at 0430 hours next morning. At times during the night fire was coming from three directions: the only direction from which fire was not received being from High Wall. The situation was not pleasant as there were several places where the Turks could collect before attempting to rush the mound—notably in the arch itself and in Suliman Pak village. This village was occupied by the Turks early in the night, and at times bodies penetrated into the arch. During the whole night the shouts of the Turks were heard, evidently trying to persuade their men to advance and rush the mound. The fire discipline of the Battalion was steady and controlled throughout the night. A message was sent to the Water Redoubt by Captain Haig, asking for artillery fire to be turned on to Suliman Pak village, where it was obvious that the Turks had collected in considerable numbers. The reply, however, was received that it was not considered advisable to bombard the village on account of the sacred tomb situated therein. Arrangements were, however, made for fire to be brought down between the village and arch on demand. At times this worked fairly well.

At dawn large numbers of the enemy were seen streaming away from our positions towards the river and their bridge of boats. It has subsequently been ascertained from Turkish sources that they attempted a great counter-attack during this night, and that the whole of the 35th Turkish Division was endeavouring to capture Gurkha Mound. Their best, and recently arrived, Division, the 51st, was to attack Vital Point but lost its way in the dark, went round in circles and never came into action, except for small bodies. The resistance of the Gurkha Mound detachment in which the 24th Punjabis gallantly played its part can best be described by an extract from the Turkish point of view, quoted in the British Official History of the campaign :—

"The 35th Division strove for hours in front of that brave and determined little force left alone on the little hill-top, and though it lost many men did not gain its end. They did not succeed in drawing near even."

The Turkish writer then goes on to say that he met Captain Stockley after the fall of Kut, who, having been on Gurkha Mound in charge of a machine-gun battery, told the Turkish historian the British point of view. The Turkish historian then proceeds :—

"According to him, that detachment consisted of 100 men of the 24th Punjabis and 300 men of the 2nd/7th Gurkhas, and a machine-gun company, under the command of the brave and daring Lieut.-Colonel Powell, commanding the 2nd/7th Gurkhas. Having listened, with a forced politeness and a disdain I was far from feeling in reality, I must confess to a deep hidden feeling of appreciation of the deed of that brave self-sacrificing enemy detachment, which for hours, though only 400 strong, opposed and finally drove back the thousands of riflemen of the 35th Division to the second line of defence."

The above account brings to an end the work of the 24th Punjabis during the two days' fighting on November 22nd and 23rd, 1915. Although the result of the battle was a tactical victory, yet the losses of the British force were such that subsequent retreat was inevitable. It was an extremely gallantly fought fight and a great feat of arms, in that somewhat under 14,000 British and Indian troops defeated more than 20,000 Turks in an entrenched and well-prepared position. The men of the Battalion engaged more than upheld the previous proud traditions of the Regiment. In addition to the strain of the two days' fighting the men suffered from the very inadequate commissariat arrangements. The first food received after leaving Lajj was a bag full of cooked chupattis, sufficient to provide each man with one chupatti. This food was not received until the morning of November 24th. The men were not able to have a proper meal until the morning of November 26th, after arrival back in Lajj. Lack of water was also severely felt during the two days of the actual battle.

The following rewards were given to the British officers engaged:—

>Brevet Colonel S. H. Climo: C.B.
>Lieut.-Colonel H. A. V. Cummins: Brevet Colonel.
>Captain A. B. Haig: Military Cross.
>Captain R. C. Clifford (I.M.S.): D.S.O.

Lieutenant H. C. Dillon would undoubtedly have been singled out for reward had he survived.

Owing to the paucity of, and casualties among, the British officers, it is probable that a good many deeds of gallantry passed unseen.

The following, however, were among the rewards given to the Indian ranks:—

>Jemadar Pirthi Chand: I.D.S.M.
>4375 Havildar Sundar Singh, 514 Lance-Naik Pal Singh, and 4358 Naik Gusaun: I.O.M.
>4755 Naik Labh Singh and 383 Sepoy Lal Singh: I.D.S.M.

The casualties of the 24th Punjabis during these two days were:—

>*Killed.*—2 British officers, 2 Indian officers, 25 Indian other ranks.
>*Wounded.*—2 British officers, 4 Indian officers, 144 Indian other ranks.
>*Missing.*—43 Indian other ranks.

This was a loss of 65 per cent. of the numbers engaged. There is no doubt that the missing were either killed or died of wounds. None were heard of as having been taken prisoner.

Before daylight on November 24th orders were received for the detachment on Gurkha Mound to withdraw to High Wall. The Maxim Battery and the 2nd/7th Gurkhas left first, followed by the 24th Punjabis. At 0745 hours the Battalion left the mound and arrived at High Wall twenty minutes later. The Battalion now rejoined its permanent brigade (30th) and came under the command of Major-General Melliss, V.C., once more. The remainder of the day was spent in entrenching High Wall, and the time passed quietly. The Turks had, in fact, withdrawn to the Diyala River. During November 25th the British force gradually concentrated at High Wall. All the transport was collected under the shelter of the wall, and was very crowded. During the day the Turks began to advance, and the

British positions were shelled intermittently but with remarkably little damage. On reports being received during the afternoon of the advance from the Diyala of three Turkish columns, General Townshend decided to retire. As there had been a good number of casualties among the transport, and as the majority of the A.T. Carts were employed in evacuating the wounded, it was impossible to remove all the ammunition. Accordingly a large number of boxes were buried. All ammunition in regimental charge was actually removed. Although orders were issued at about 1700 hours for an immediate march to Lajj there was much delay in moving off in the dark, and the 30th Brigade which had the post of honour in the rear did not get on the move until 2000 hours. The Battalion formed the right flank guard. The column eventually reached Lajj at midnight, November 25th–26th, the march having been unmolested.

On November 26th Captain A. C. H. Trevor rejoined, as his Motor Machine Gun Section had been broken up, and took over command from Captain Haig. November 26th was a day of rest, and the whole force remained at Lajj. On the 27th the retirement was continued, the force moving off from Lajj in the afternoon. The 30th Brigade was again rearguard to the whole force. Aziziya was reached at 0800 hours on November 28th, after a tiring march of 23 miles through the afternoon and night. A curious incident occurred at dawn shortly before reaching Aziziya. Sniping shots were fired from a distance of about 700 yards at the column. A party of the 24th Punjabis under Captain Haig were sent out to deal with and drive off the snipers. A figure was seen running away on the advance of this party, and fire was opened at 600 yards range. After a few rounds the figure fell. On advancing to see the "bag" a very frightened but unhurt Gurkha recruit of the 2nd/7th Gurkhas was found. He had evidently strayed from the column during the night, lost his head and opened fire.

Animal transport was now very limited and as much kit as possible was put on board supply and transport barges at Aziziya. The barge on which the battalion kit and records was loaded was, unfortunately, sunk during the action of December 1st. Among other things all war diaries, regimental pay records and field treasure chest accounts were lost. Captain A. O. Sutherland now took over command, as the wing at Aziziya rejoined.

The Arabs, so friendly on our march up to Ctesiphon, had now become hostile, in their usual treacherous way. General Nixon, the commander of I.E.F. "D," who had been present at the Battle of Ctesiphon, was now on his way down to Basra by steamer. The river line of communication was unsafe and General Nixon's ship had been held up in the vicinity of Kut. The 30th Brigade was, accordingly, ordered to march ahead of the main force and to open up the lines of communication near Kut. About 0800 hours on November 30th the Brigade marched twenty miles towards Kut. The 33rd Cavalry and the 1st/5th Hants Territorial Field Battery (four howitzers) accompanied the Brigade. A certain amount of trouble was given by the Arabs on the far (right) bank of the river, when watering operations were in progress. An Arab village was accordingly shelled by the battery, with good results. The remainder of the Force marched from Aziziya later in the day but only proceeded as far as ten miles from that place.

At 0630 hours on December 1st, when the Brigade was just about to fall in to continue its march towards Kut, two officers arrived from General Townshend with the news that the Turks had caught up the 6th Division, that the latter had been shelled during the night, and would be attacked in the morning. The 30th Brigade thereupon was ordered to retrace its steps and go to the help of the 6th Division. This involved a march back towards Aziziya of seven miles. By about 0930 hours the Brigade, in which was now incorporated Headquarters and half a battalion of the 2nd Battalion Queen's Own Royal West Kent Regiment, had taken up a rear-guard position, through which the transport and the Brigades of 6th Division passed. By the time the remainder of the force had passed through the Turks had advanced up to about 600 yards from the 30th Brigade's line; 2nd Queen's Own Royal West Kent Regiment being on the left and the 24th Punjabis on the right. The two battalions retired together; the companies of the 24th Punjabis retiring in extended order and covering each other by fire. After the Turks had been shaken off the Battalion withdrew in lines of companies in columns of fours. For some time the Turks continued to shell the retiring Brigade, but their shrapnel was, for the most part, burst very high and caused little or no damage. Eventually only a few mounted Arabs followed up the retiring British. The march was continued all day up to midnight. It was a most exhausting march, the distance covered up to midnight being 34 miles, *i.e.*, seven miles more than the 6th Division had marched. The battle casualties were few—only eight men wounded—but the physically weak found the march a great strain. This applied specially to the draft from the 123rd Outram's Rifles, many of whom had to be forcibly kept on the move and prevented from straggling. The Dogra Company, under Jemadar Pirthi Chand, specially distinguished itself during this trying march by its excellent discipline and perfect formation. The only halt during this day was one of an hour's duration at about 1700 hours. At midnight a point some twenty miles from Kut, called Monkey Village by the force, was reached. Here there was to have been a halt of two hours, but actually the troops did not move on until 0500 hours on December 2nd. Some food was cooked here for the men, while the officers secured some tinned pineapple and biscuits, this being the only food that had been eaten since the early morning. The march was continued at 0500 hours. Although the Turks had been outdistanced and were no longer interfering with the retirement the progress made was not quick. There was a certain amount of trouble from Arabs on the opposite bank, usually when the troops went to the river for water. A two-hours' halt was made at 1300 hours, when the opportunity was taken to remove boots and relieve sore feet. Eventually, at dusk, the force bivouacked some three miles from Kut. Food and blankets were sent out from this place, arriving about midnight.

At dawn on December 3rd the force continued its march into Kut. Thus ended a memorable retreat, in the course of which the Battalion covered 74 miles in three days, and this, for half the Battalion, on the top of a very exhausting ten days. It was a performance to be proud of.

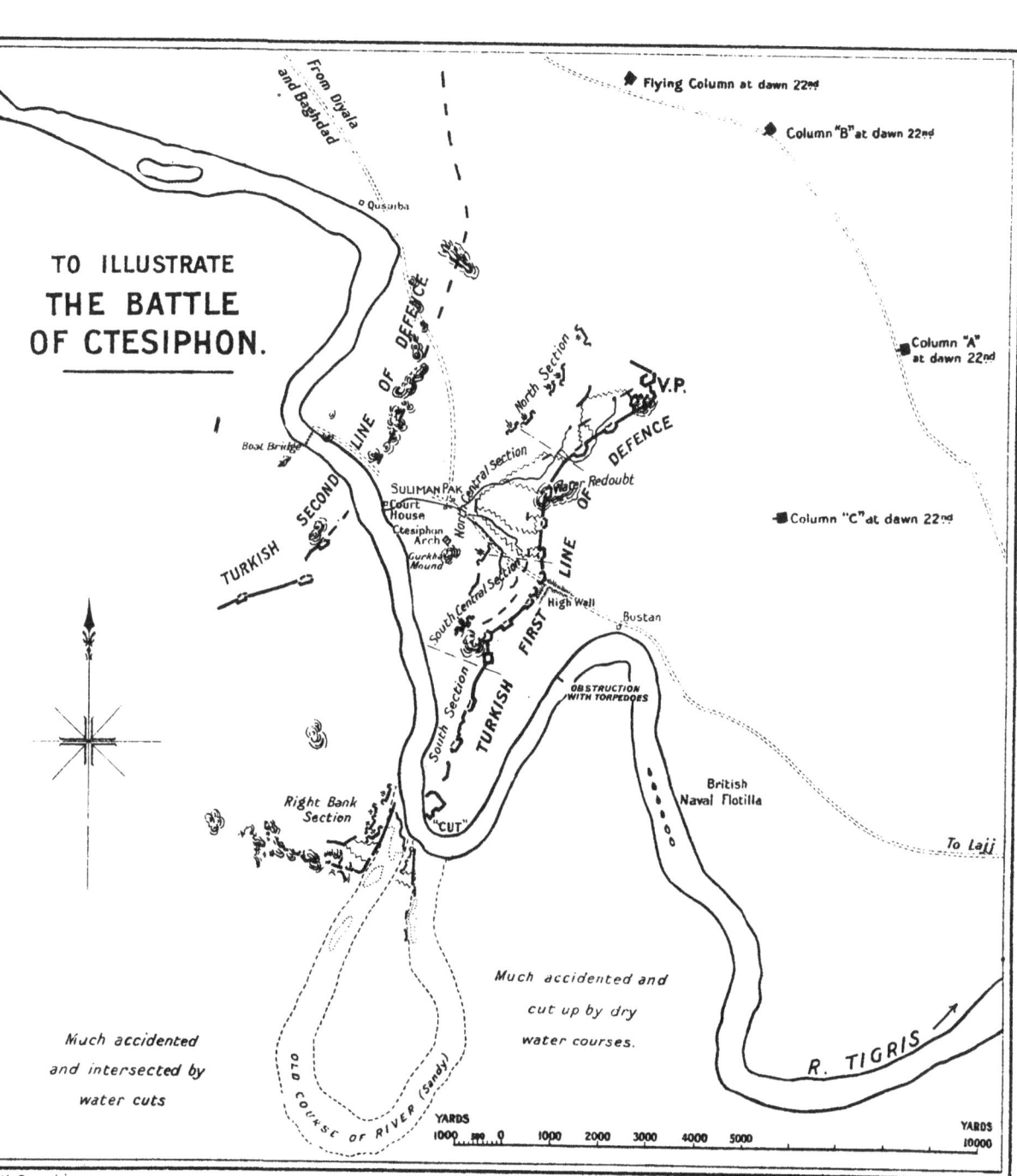

CHAPTER V.

THE SIEGE OF KUT.

ON arrival in Kut, Brigades were told off to various sectors. The 30th Brigade was retained in the town as general reserve. Later in the day the Battalion was ordered into billets in the outskirts of the town. This involved turning out the Arab inhabitants, who only withdrew with their impedimenta after a good deal of forcible persuasion. On this day Lieut.-Colonel Cummins rejoined and took over command, and Captain Sutherland returned to his own unit, the 22nd Punjabis.

On December 4th the billets were cleaned up, walls knocked down to provide communication throughout, and the outer walls loopholed. Arrangements were also made for falling in at the shortest notice, and company and battalion assembly positions decided upon.

Prior to the arrival of Townshend's force in Kut there were no trenches. The place was defended as a post on the lines of communication. The defences consisted of a "Fort," built of mud, and four block-houses, coloured white. These block-houses were connected by a single line of wire. The defences were only intended to keep out small bands of marauding Arabs. As no trenches existed these had to be dug, and eventually over twenty miles of trenches were excavated. The first task of the 30th Brigade was the construction of the second line. The trace of this line was laid out and digging begun on December 5th. The sector allotted to the 24th Punjabis was 500 yards westwards from the river, the 2nd/7th Gurkhas continuing on the left. The general line of this trench ran a little in front (*i.e.*, north) of the Brick Kilns, which was our main artillery position during the siege. On December 6th the 6th Cavalry Brigade left Kut, crossing to the right bank by a bridge near the Fort and proceeding down to Amara.

On December 7th, about 1830 hours, orders were received to proceed immediately to the Fort. The Battalion was on the move in twenty minutes and arrived at the Fort at 2000 hours. There being no transport all reserve ammunition had to be man-handled. On arrival at the Fort orders were given for the Battalion to proceed outside the front line trench and seize and hold (in conjunction with the 22nd Punjabis) a water-cut some 500 yards distant, which the Turks had held during the day and from which they had been worrying the sappers engaged in dismantling the bridge of boats. The two Battalions advanced in three lines, in echelon from the right: 1st line, half 22nd Punjabis; 2nd line, half 22nd and half 24th

Punjabis; 3rd line, half 24th Punjabis. The operation was successfully carried out and without opposition, as the Turks retired. The only incident was that fire was opened on the 24th Punjabis by mistake by an Indian unit of the 17th Brigade, which unit apparently had not been informed of the impending operation.

The two battalions remained in occupation of the water-cut for the greater part of the night, which was a bitterly cold one, until the bridge was successfully dismantled. Billets were reached at 0400 hours on December 8th. The bridge was again constructed up-stream of the second line, and a double company of the 67th Punjabis put across the river on the right bank to form a bridge head. On the morning of December 9th this double company was heavily attacked and driven across the river, leaving a certain number of casualties on the far bank. About 1100 hours on this day the Battalion was hurriedly ordered out to the river bank near the bridge. The situation then was that the Turks held the far bank, the British the near bank, and there was an intact bridge spanning the river. Moreover, if the Turks managed to force a crossing here, their lodgment on the British bank would have been in rear of all our defences. However, the Turks made no serious attempt to cross. There was desultory firing all day on both sides.

It was decided to blow up the bridge after dark. This was successfully accomplished by Lieutenant A. B. Mathews, Royal Engineers, and Lieutenant R. Sweet, 2nd/7th Gurkhas. The Battalion was in readiness to open heavy covering fire on the opposite bank, in the event of the Turks attempting to interfere with the demolition. The bridge was blown up in two places, thus dividing the bridge into three parts. The only portion recovered by us was that nearest to our bank. The loss of this bridge thus early in the siege, undoubtedly had a very serious bearing on the subsequent fate of the Kut Garrison: for the best and quickest means of crossing the river and so of being able to co-operate with the relieving force was thus destroyed. A party of forty rifles of the Battalion, under Subadar Jhanda Singh, was now ordered to go across the river in a launch and attempt to recover the wounded (including a British officer) of the 67th Punjabis, who had been left on the far bank. When the party had been assembled, however, the order was cancelled and a party of the 67th Punjabis was ordered across to pick up their own wounded. The Turks had evidently been drawn back to the river bank by the noise of the blowing up of the bridge, and the launch was so heavily fired upon as it crossed the river that it had to withdraw. This ended the day's operations and the Battalion returned to billets at midnight.

It is not possible now to give a daily diary of events. Accordingly the account will be divided into periods in which the work done was almost the same daily.

December 10th to December 25th.

During this period the second line trench and all the communication trenches were completed or commenced. It was not possible to work on a shallow trench by day from about the beginning of this period. The men worked four hours by day and four hours by night at entrenching, and the night was always spent in the second line trench. The Regiment returned to billets soon after dawn, after standing to. There were usually a few casualties daily, chiefly from " overs " which all fell about the second line trench and brick kilns. Towards the end of this period the 30th Brigade relieved the 16th Brigade in the front line (north-west section). There was, however, an extra regiment now in the Brigade, which was composed of Headquarters and half The Queen's Own Royal West Kent Regiment, one Company 1st/4th Hampshire Regiment (T.F.), 7th Gurkhas, 24th and 76th Punjabis, and half the 67th Punjabis. Only four regiments were required, and the 24th were left out of the front line owing to the distrust felt by all commanders of Afridis. Consequently, when the 30th Brigade went in the front line the 24th came under the orders of the 16th Brigade and remained in General Reserve the whole time. The 30th and 16th Brigades remained for a week at a time in the front line. A heavy attack was made by the Turks on the Fort on Christmas Eve but the position was maintained. The result of this attack was that a new trench, called the " New Retrenchment," was dug from Redoubt " B " to the river eastwards, to which the garrison of the Fort could retire in case of necessity. Otherwise the capture of the Fort would have meant the loss of most of the front line.

The Battalion had a strong working party under Captain A. C. H. Trevor to start the digging of the New Retrenchment. The work was carried out under considerable fire.

December 26th to January 21st.

December 26th was the first night on which the Regiment had a rest from digging since the commencement of the siege. The men at this time were getting exhausted from much digging. During this period the Regiment used to go up and occupy the New Retrenchment as " Close Reserve " about five times a week. On the other two nights there were probably working parties of 200 men. There were also frequent working parties by day, finishing and deepening communication trenches. On a New Retrenchment night the Regiment formed up at dusk and proceeded by the various communication trenches to the New Retrenchment, a distance of nearly two miles. A party of fifty rifles was then sent on to Redoubt " A " as a support to the 22nd Punjabis (Afridis were not allowed in this party). When fully light, and after standing to for an hour before dawn, the Regiment returned in the same way to billets.

On the night of January 20th-21st there was heavy rain, which resulted in the abandonment of most of the front line trenches by both the Turks and ourselves. Many Turks were killed while retiring. The Regiment was in the New Retrenchment on this night and parties had to be sent off to help to construct bunds, etc. On going down Gurkha communication trench the water was found to get deeper and deeper. Finally it came half-way up the thigh, so an attempt was made to go back over the open. But immediately the first men appeared out of the trench a heavy fire was opened which resulted in several casualties. Accordingly the march back was resumed in the trench.

January 22nd to March 7th.

The result of the rain on the night of January 20th-21st was that our front line could only be held from the river (on the right) to Redoubt " B " (inclusive). Thence our front line was the middle line trench to the river on the left. Up to January 21st the two front lines had been only forty yards apart in some places and there was more or less continuous fire day and night. During the period up to January 21st one could count at night the noise of thirty to sixty rifle shots per minute. It was the same during the day, but at night the noise was naturally heard more clearly. This all ceased after January 21st and the cessation of noise was a very distinct relief. During most of the siege the Turks bombarded the place daily. Usually in the evening, but often also in the morning.

To fill the gap between Redoubt " B " and the middle line, three trenches (called the echelon trenches) were dug. These were occupied by a party from the " Close Reserve " Regiment at night. The work in this period was much the same as in the preceding period, but perhaps somewhat lighter. Up to January 21st there were usually three battalions in " Close Reserve," but in this period there was only one—in the New Retrenchment. During this period (especially the latter part) the working parties were chiefly engaged in the construction of bunds in view of the annual floods which were expected about the middle of March. At the beginning of this period British officers and other ranks were first issued with horse or mule flesh daily. The bread ration was about eight ounces, but Indian ranks (except Gurkhas) refused to eat horse-flesh at this time and were given preferential treatment as regards atta, obtaining more than British troops. There was no real fighting during this period, but a considerable amount of sniping on both sides. The Battalion machine guns (without Afridis) were in the front line, and a sniping detachment was also formed.

March 8th to 9th.

About 0200 hours on March 8th the Regiment marched from billets to the transport lines, and formed up under cover with the remainder of the 30th Brigade (less 67th Punjabis) in readiness to cross the river in the event of General Aylmer's relieving force having any success in the attempt to capture the Dujaila Redoubt. The Afridis were again left out and were sent to the Serai. The crossing was to be made on the tug *Samana*, to which two barges were attached. Four hundred men could cross at a time. The first portion of the Regiment was to cross on the third trip. The Brigade remained all day hidden in the transport lines but unfortunately General Aylmer's attack was unsuccessful. The Brigade returned to billets about 1800 hours, and early next morning went out again to " 5th Avenue " (a street in the town) in case General Aylmer should renew his attack. The failure of this attempt was a great disappointment to the men. They had all spent money in buying themselves extra food, in order to make themselves as strong as possible for any fighting that might have taken place. In spite of this all ranks still had no doubts as to being relieved ultimately.

March 10th to April 29th.

Rations were now reduced. All horses and mules over and above what were required for food were shot in order to save grain. The preferential treatment of Indian ranks as regards atta was stopped, and they now received the same amount as British ranks. But for a time they still refused to eat horse-flesh.

Telegrams (by wireless) were sent to the Golden Temple Amritsar for the Sikhs, to the Jama Musjid, Delhi, for Mussalmans, and to a big Hindu Pandit for the Hindus: all asking if, in the special circumstances, there was any objection to the eating of horse-flesh. The answers received were favourable, but for a time this made no difference to the troops. At length when the atta ration was reduced to five ounces all ranks gave in, saying they could not carry on with that amount of food. Before the end (for about a fortnight or three weeks) the atta ration was as little as four ounces.

The annual floods arrived about March 15th. As a result Redoubt " B " and the New Retrenchment were flooded and had to be abandoned. The Battalion in " Close Reserve " was therefore sent every night to the second line. Eventually this was given up and battalions so detailed remained in their billets in a state of readiness.

It was also thought possible that the enemy might attempt to cross the river from the neighbourhood of the Hai, and a battalion was always detailed nightly to be held in readiness to support the river piquets from second line to the town. Working parties were still required, but not so frequently towards the end. The work was nearly always in connection with flood protection. A large parapet was made in the middle line trench and this fortunately held. The flood water extended right up to the middle line. Sniping was still continued on both sides, and also the daily Turkish bombardment. In addition we were bombed by the two Turkish or German aeroplanes with which our machines from the relieving force appeared unable to cope. The regimental billets were only hit once with a bomb. In this we were fortunate, as favourite targets of the enemy machines were the Brick Kilns (where the majority of our guns were concentrated) and the transport lines, both of these being quite close to the regimental billets.

Our aeroplanes nevertheless succeeded in dropping a certain amount of food; sufficient to feed the garrison for four days. The *Julnar* (river steamer) attempted to run the blockade on the night of April 25th-26th. Working parties of 200 men each from the 24th Punjabis and the 7th Gurkhas were detailed to unload the *Julnar* on arrival. Covering parties were detailed to keep down the enemy's fire from the opposite bank, and our guns were ready to fire on the enemy's batteries. The ship was timed to reach the bank close to the Fort at midnight, and about that time a very heavy fire of guns, rifles, and machine guns was heard from the direction of Magasis. This continued for a quarter of an hour and then ceased suddenly. The ship did not arrive, and finally the working parties returned to billets at 0300 hours. It was only after this failure that the majority of the garrison realized that there was no longer any hope of their being relieved.

On the night of April 28th-29th the destruction of war material commenced. Small arms ammunition was either thrown into the river or burnt on the morning of April 29th.

All machine guns, rifles, and equipment of every sort was burnt on the morning of April 29th, a small proportion of rifles being kept in the front line. The guns were destroyed on the 29th. The Turks obtained nothing of military value from the Battalion. Turkish troops marched in through the Fort about midday. At 1400 hours the 30th Brigade embarked on a Turkish river steamer and was conveyed up the river to Shumran Camp, arriving at 2000 hours. The whole force was collected there by the evening of the 31st. On May 7th the men were separated from the officers and marched off to Baghdad. Promises were obtained from the commander of the escort as regards short marches and good treatment. Unfortunately the character of the Turk was not realized at this time and so the officers were comparatively easy in their minds in connection with the men's treatment at the moment of their departure.

The regimental casualties during the siege were as follows:—

Killed.—16 Indian ranks, 2 followers.

Died of Wounds.—11 Indian ranks.

Wounded.—96 Indian ranks, 2 followers.

Missing.—2 Indian ranks.

Died of Disease.—11 Indian ranks, 4 followers.

Total.—144.

This does not include deaths from disease in April, which were fairly heavy, nor three deaths from disease in the Turkish Camp at Shumran.

The totals for the whole force up to March 31st were:—

Killed.—8 British officers, 6 Indian officers, 84 British ranks, 343 Indian ranks, and 63 followers.

Died of Wounds.—9 British officers, 7 Indian officers, 103 British ranks, 263 Indian ranks, and 72 followers.

Wounded.—44 British officers, 19 Indian officers, 343 British ranks 1,171 Indian ranks, and 259 followers.

Missing.—1 British officer, 1 Indian officer, 2 British ranks, 41 Indian ranks, and 3 followers.

Died of Disease.—2 British officers, 3 Indian officers, 36 British ranks, 418 Indian ranks, and 87 followers.

Total.—3,388.

Deaths from disease in April were heavy, there being few medicines and very little milk, etc. Acute enteritis was rampant at the end.

There was a certain amount of desertion towards the end of the siege. Only two of the Battalion deserted, both Afridis. Desertion was not, however, entirely confined to Mohammedans, and there were cases of Sikhs and Hindus deserting. To check desertion all sentries were doubled. One Hindu or Sikh, and one Mohammedan. A case occurred in one unit in which the Mohammedan of such a sentry post deserted, and the Hindu with him was shot for allowing it.

To complete the account of the Siege of Kut a few general reflections will be made. First and foremost comes the matter of food, which must ever be of vital importance to a beleaguered force, affecting not only its health, stamina and morale, but also the duration of the defence. It cannot be said that, in the light of after events anyhow, the food question was satisfactorily handled. Rations were kept at a comparatively high scale up to March 8th or thereabouts. After this date there was a big drop. From the hygienic and scientific point of view a more gradual reduction would have had better effects. Then there was the grave question of the eating of horse-flesh by Indian ranks. No amount of persuasion would induce them to eat horse-flesh until the grain ration was cut so low that the men felt that they simply could not exist on it. Their objections (and this applies to the whole of the Indian ranks of the Force) were that they feared that there would be social boycott when they returned to their homes; that they would be outcasted and that no one would give them their daughters in marriage. To give an order, which clearly would not be obeyed, would not have met the case. The only solution would appear to have been not to give Indian ranks preferential treatment in the matter of atta. There is no doubt that failure to eat horse-flesh undermined the strength of the men, and they were not as robust as they might have been, or, to put it another way, they were weaker than they need have been. In the end this probably did not make very much difference from a fighting point of view, because the men were strong enough to have made what effort was required of them on March 8th, had they been called on for this effort. After March 8th there was little hope of relief, and certainly after that date there was little chance of any useful co-operation by the garrison, mainly because of the floods and secondly because of the rapidly increasing debilitation of the men, British as well as Indian. After March 8th the men were not getting a ration containing sufficient vitamins to replace the daily wastage in the body. Consequently they were slowly starving; and this continued for just over seven weeks.

The conditions in the hospitals were very bad. Medicines and medical comforts were scarce or non-existent, and food such as eggs and milk was almost impossible to obtain. All available supplies in the town were, of course, bought for the use of the hospitals, but it was very insufficient. Stomach diseases were the most prevalent, and men wasted away for lack of proper food. For instance, there was a man of the Battalion in hospital whose thigh was literally no thicker than an ordinary man's wrist. Visits to the hospitals were always depressing affairs. General Townshend practically never visited his troops in the line or town. He visited, however, the hospitals frequently. This may account for his erroneous impressions of the morale of his Indian troops. Considering all things, their morale remained as high as could be expected, thanks to the close touch kept with the men by the British officers.

The saddest reflection of all is that had it not been for errors of judgment on the part of various commanders Kut need never have fallen, and some 12,000 men, British and Indian, would not have become prisoners of war in the hands of the Turks for over two years, during which time nearly 70 per cent. of the British ranks and 25 per cent. of the Indian ranks perished through gross ill-treatment and mismanagement on the part of the Turks. This conduct of the Turks should never be forgiven or forgotten.

The numbers of the Battalion who were captured at the fall of Kut were: 9 British officers (including Medical Officer), 13 Indian officers, 457 Indian other ranks, and 34 followers.

The names of the British officers were:—

    Lieutenant-Colonel H. A. V. Cummins, Commanding.
    Captain A. C. H. Trevor, Second-in-Command.
    Captain A. B. Haig, Adjutant.
    Lieutenant W. W. A. Phillips, I.A.R.O.
    Lieutenant H. Duxbury, I.A.R.O.
    Lieutenant Stapleton, I.A.R.O.
    Lieutenant H. Browne, I.A.R.O.
    Captain R. C. Clifford, I.M.S.

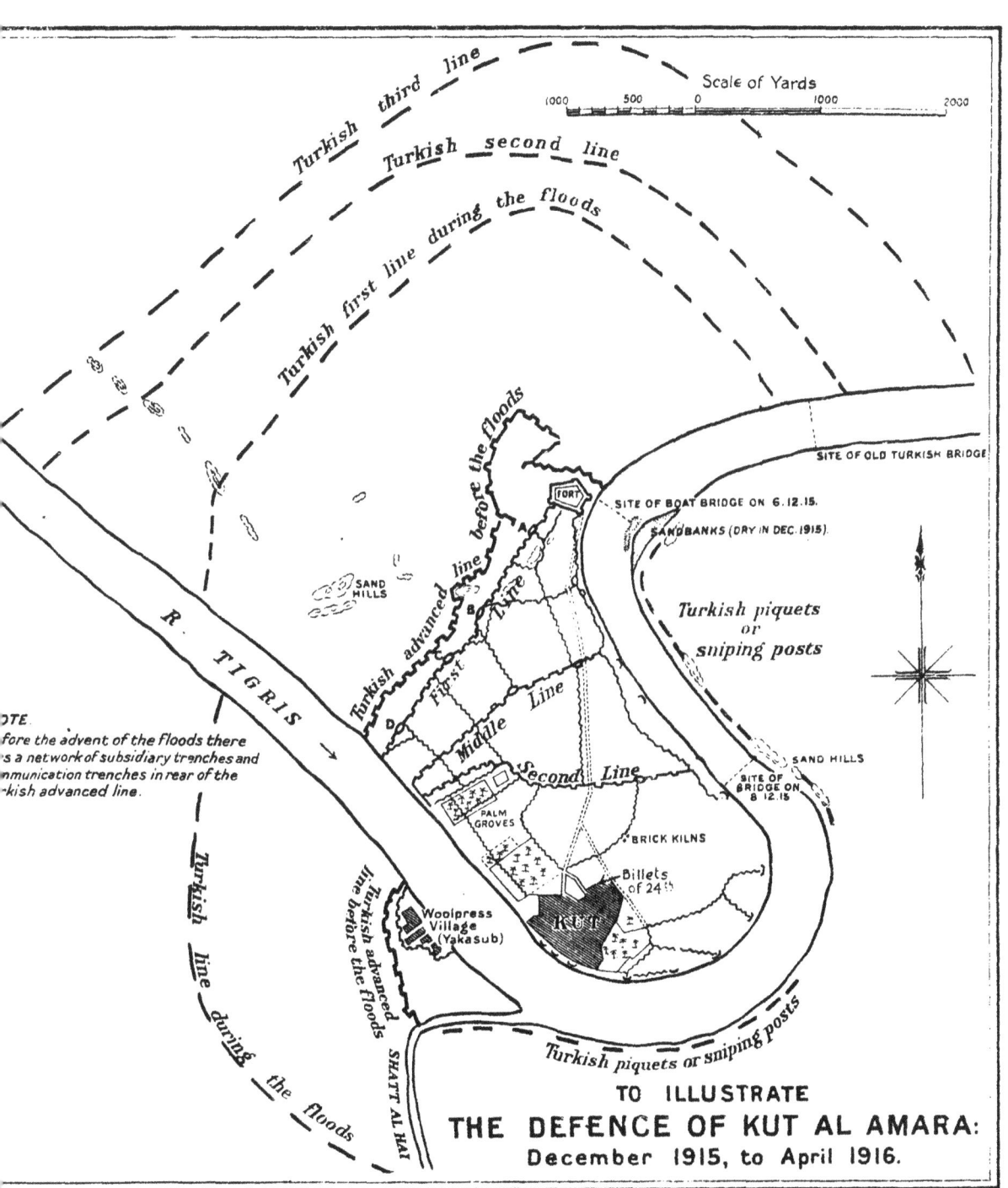

Captain C. A. Bignell, 4th Rajputs, was never fit for duty during the siege. He eventually died in 1916 as a prisoner at Yozgad.

The names of the Indian officers were:—

"A" Company.—Subedar Ghulam Mahomed and Jemadar Sher Baz.
"B" Company.—Subedar Kishen Singh and Jemadar Sawan Singh.
"C" Company.—Subedar Lal Mir and Jemadar Sher Nur.
"D" Company.—Subedar Jhanda Singh.
"E" Company.—Jemadars Pirthi Chand and Nathu.
"F" Company.—Subedar Umar Khan.
"G" Company.—Subedar-Major Diwan Singh and Jemadar Bhola Singh.
"H" Company.—Jemadar Narain Singh.

The casualties suffered by the Battalion given above were more than the average suffered by other battalions. Located as the Battalion was on the outskirts of the town there was a steady flow of daily casualties, chiefly from overs, and occasionally from shelling.

The defence of Kut, though it had an unfortunate ending, was yet a very gallant feat of arms on the part of the garrison, and the Battalion carried out all the work allotted to it with cheerfulness and with spirit. It is only fitting then that one of the battle honours earned by the Battalion should be "The Defence of Kut-el-Amara."

CHAPTER VI.

THE BATTALION IN CAPTIVITY.

BEFORE continuing with the story of the reconstitution of the Battalion and its subsequent career during the remainder of the Great War, a brief account will be given of the experiences of the British and Indian officers and of the Indian other ranks during their captivity.

British Officers.

The other ranks left Shumran Camp on May 7th, and the British and Indian officers were left alone in the camp. On May 12th they embarked in the s.s. *Basra* after at least one false alarm, and proceeded by river to Baghdad. On the way the salved s.s. *Julnar*, which had attempted to run the blockade, was passed. Her funnels were literally like sieves, riddled with bullet holes. The *Basra* tied up for the night near Ctesiphon. Arabs came down to the bank to express their pleasure at the capture of the British and to show by signs how they would like to treat them, *i.e.*, by cutting their throats. These were the same Arabs who had expressed their pleasure at our advance a few months before. On the 13th the city of Baghdad was reached. The officers disembarked at the former British Consulate. All officers of the rank of captain or below were then formed up in procession, in file, and had thus to march through the main streets of Baghdad to impress the populace with the Turkish victory. It must at once be said that the populace displayed no signs of hostility. They appeared rather to be sorry for our plight. Eventually the officers' destination, the cavalry barracks, north of Baghdad, was reached. Here the officers were rather crowded up, considering the space available, and the first taste, or rather smell, of Turkish sanitation was experienced. Words cannot express the revolting state of the latrines, and this was found to be the same in every Turkish barrack that was occupied by the British. Most officers were feeling weak from their previous privations, and there was a considerable amount of sickness, serious and otherwise. Money was a difficulty. The Turks never provided the British officers with rations. However, each officer had been issued with about four gold liras before the surrender, and the Turks gave a month's pay in Baghdad, amounting, for a captain, to seven or eight liras. This money was paid in gold and was the last money in coin that was destined to be seen.

The officers were now divided up into two echelons, each numbering roughly 100, excluding the Generals and most of the staff, who proceeded to Brusa. These 200 officers were the only ones fit to travel. Any sick ones were left in Baghdad and came up by degrees to Asia Minor. On May 16th all entrained at the station and proceeded to Samara, arriving about midnight. They were then sent to the Serai on the river bank, about a mile distant from the station. At this place a halt was made until the first echelon started for Mosul, and while transport was collected for the second echelon in which the fit officers of the Battalion were included. The only fit officers were Captains Trevor and Haig, and Lieutenant Browne, *i.e.*, three out of eight officers, excluding the Medical Officer. In due course the march to Mosul started. Kit was very limited; transport was scarcer still. Mosul was reached on May 30th, after a nine days' march. This march was trying, water was frequently scarce, and food consisted largely of chupattis and dates, which had been bought in Baghdad. In Mosul the barracks were occupied. The conditions were the same as in Baghdad. The officers were, however, allowed out to a restaurant at which cooked food was available at very expensive prices. Transport, hitherto, had consisted of donkeys. From Mosul to Ras-el-Ain carts, the country "arabieh," were provided. Mosul was left on June 2nd and Ras-el-Ain reached on June 10th. The conditions under which the officers marched were extremely galling. No Turk in authority could or would say how long the marches were to be; the column went on until ordered to stop, sometimes marching by day, sometimes all night. In the same way as on the march to Mosul food had to be bought beforehand for the whole march of roughly ten days' duration.

At Ras-el-Ain the railhead of the Baghdad railway was reached. The echelon then proceeded by train to Aleppo, where the officers were distributed among various small hotels in the town, paying for their accommodation. Food was difficult to obtain, and the gendarmes, under whose escort the officers now were, were extremely pig-headed, obstinate, and generally objectionable. After a stay of three days at Aleppo the train was once more taken, this time for Islahie at the foot of the Amanus range. The tunnelling necessary to pass the railway through this range had not yet been completed and a two days' march by road was necessary to cross the mountains. Here were seen the second signs of Armenian massacres. Two columns of Armenians were observed being hounded along the road by Turkish or Kurdish guards. Dead Armenians from these columns were seen dotted along the road. The first signs of Armenian massacres had been seen when approaching Nisibin. Whole villages in this area had been wiped out and several wells were discovered filled with dead Armenians. At Mamourie on the North of the Amanus the railway carried the second echelon across the Cilician Plains through

Adana to Gulek, at the foot of the Taurus Mountains. Here again the tunnelling operations were not complete. Instead of marching, the officers and their kit were placed on German motor lorries, driven by Germans, of whom there was a large camp half-way across the range.

It should be mentioned here that any Germans met with on the journey did their best for the British officers. It was quite obvious also that there was great friction between them and the Turks. Both nationalities told the British how objectionable or how hopeless to deal with, as the case might be, was the other nation.

A run of some forty-five miles through the Cilician gates brought the officers to Bozanti. Here the train was taken for the last time, and in due course Angora was reached via Konia and Eski Chehir. All Hindus or Sikhs who had accompanied the officers either as orderlies or servants had been detained at Ras-el-Ain. At Eski Chehir all Mohammedans were also stopped. There were already at this place a certain number of Mohammedan Indian officers.

At Angora the first and second echelons of the British officers met. After three or four extremely uncomfortable days spent in a large and gaunt building on the outskirts of the town the second echelon left for Kastamoni, the first echelon proceeding to Yozgad. The pleasantest part of the whole journey was that between Angora and Kastamoni. The commander of the escort was helpful and obliging and kept his men in order. The scenery was pleasant and the marches of reasonable length. Kastamoni was the headquarters of a " vilayet." It was a town of some 30,000 inhabitants situated in a valley among undulating downs at a height of about 3,000 feet. The climate, taken all the year round, was not unlike that of a Himalayan hill station in India. It was found unnecessary to wear " topis." The officers, on arrival, were distributed in various empty houses in the Greek quarter of the town. More officers, who had been left behind sick, gradually arrived during the autumn, extra houses being taken over for their accommodation. The officers began to settle down to their routine life, which was exceedingly dull. Naturally the feeling uppermost in everyone's mind was one of extreme disappointment at being out of any further share in the war, so far as could be foreseen.

To begin with the Turkish staff of the camp were irritating to a degree, orders and regulations of a petty and useless nature being issued. However, by the exercise of tact and good handling, conditions of life became reasonable, but not before the original Turkish commandant had been removed for malpractices concerning money affairs. Money was a great difficulty. The pay of a captain was seven liras a month. Eventually three to five liras a month were distributed through the Red Crescent Society, working in conjunction with the Red Cross Society. But it was still necessary to cash cheques. This was mostly done at Kastamoni through the good offices of a rich Greek merchant, who cashed cheques at a rate of 180 piastres to the pound, whereas the rate given by the neutral embassies was only 120 piastres to the pound. As the " par " rate, pre-war, was 110 to the pound, this was absurd. Paper money rapidly depreciated, as much as five paper liras being obtainable for one gold lira. The officers had to supply their own food, this being bought in the town and cooked by the British orderlies, who were allowed at the rate of one to four officers. The Turks provided no rations for the officers, but they did so for the orderlies.

Officers interested themselves in many and various ways. Many worked at trades, carpentering and boot repairing being the most popular and, moreover, of considerable benefit to their fellow prisoners. A string band was got together which provided interest for the performers, and a certain amount of pleasure to the audiences, when it played. Many other officers took up the study of languages. Daily walks could be taken under escort, and football was also played daily and provided much interest and healthy exercise. The field had to be rented by the officers. A chapel was improvised in which the Church of England padre held services on Sundays.

News of the outside world was difficult to obtain. The only newspapers allowed were ones published in Constantinople in either French or German. These papers contained all the enemy daily communiques in which the most was made of any enemy success, while their defeats were hardly mentioned. As an example, the Turkish communiques during March, 1917, never mentioned the capture of Baghdad by the British. What authentic news was obtained came through the medium of letters from home. As letters took anything from six weeks to four months to arrive, the news was naturally very belated. Parcels took eight months to one year to arrive. They arrived at irregular intervals, but a parcel day was a great event in the routine life of the officers. The most welcome parcels were those containing tobacco and tea.

Life thus wore on until August, 1917, when the " camp " was electrified by the escape of four officers, Lieutenants Keeling and Bishop, I.A.R.O., and Lieutenants Sweet, 7th Gurkhas, and Tipton, R.F.C. Up till then no one had considered it possible to get clear of the country, although escape from the " Camp " itself was quite feasible with careful preparation. The above party was actually recaptured by the Turks on the Black Sea coast, but was released again by some outlaws who sailed the officers and themselves across to the Crimea. Lieutenant Sweet, however, was not retaken by the outlaws and was brought back into captivity, to die in 1918 at Yozgad. As a result of this escape the Turks decided to move the camp to Kiangri, some fifty miles south of

Kastamoni, on the road to Angora. The move accordingly took place in September, 1917, and the officers were located in some disused Turkish barracks, filthy and in bad repair and emphatically quite unfit for habitation by Europeans. As a result of the complaints the Turks offered to transfer to another and better camp such as gave their parole. Much discussion followed as to whether this was permissible. The senior officers were of opinion that parole might be given; a considerable number, however, held very strong views to the contrary. In the end about seventy-five officers gave their parole and departed in December, 1917, for Gedos, far away to the south-west. About forty-four remained behind, having refused to give their parole. Most of these were maturing schemes for escaping, in view of the fact that Lieutenant Keeling's party had managed to get clear of the country. The only officers of the Battalion who remained behind at Kiangri were Captain Haig and Lieutenant Phillips who thus became separated from the remaining officers of the Battalion.

The climate of the north of Asia Minor is extremely cold during the winter. The Gedos party had a most uncomfortable journey thither, as the weather was bitter when they were passing through Afion Kara Hissar. On arrival in Gedos the officers settled down to the same sort of life as had been lived at Kastamoni and described above. They were free to go about the town and the neighbouring country within certain limits. The party left at Kiangri had a very hard winter. It was bitterly cold and snow was lying on the ground from December to the beginning of March. Firewood was very scarce, and to obtain it the officers had to buy some small trees near the barracks and cut them down themselves. The lowest temperature recorded was four degrees below zero, or 36 degrees of frost.

As the party at Kiangri had refused to give their parole they were, perhaps naturally, looked upon with suspicion by the Turks. Some of the forty-four officers had formed escape parties, and it was decided that the only way by which all could get away from the barracks was by means of a tunnel. A tunnel was accordingly begun and was nearing completion when the Turks suddenly decided to move the whole " camp " to Yozgad. The move took place in the middle of April. By the time Yozgad was reached the conditions prevailing at this " camp," which contained 100 officers were much the same as those in other " camps."

Preparations for escape were still continued by the Kiangri Party, with the addition of a very few of the older residents of the " camp." Eventually on the night of August 7th-8th, 1918, twenty-five officers broke out and started on their way in various directions towards the coast. Unfortunately all were recaptured during the ensuing ten days, except one party of eight officers. Captain Haig was a member of this party, which, after travelling some 350 miles to the South Coast of Asia Minor, succeeded in capturing a Turkish coastal motor-boat and in sailing 100 miles to Cyprus. The whole journey took thirty-seven days. For this he was awarded a bar to the Military Cross. The experiences of the party were published in a book "450 Miles to Freedom," written by two members of the party.

When the armistice with Turkey was made all the British officers from the various camps in Turkey were collected at Smyrna, from whence they were transported to Egypt and so to England.

Indian Officers.

The Indian officers accompanied the British officers to Baghdad. When the Turks distributed pay to the captured officers the Indian officers were much disturbed at their being paid at similar rates to British officers. The Turks saw that a Subedar-Major wore a crown; he was therefore paid as a major. Similarly the others were paid as lieutenants or second-lieutenants. The Indian officers feared that, if overpaid, they would have to refund the money at the end of the war. All was well, however, and they continued to receive pay at £T8 or £T7, according as to whether they were Subedars or Jemadars. Later on £T3 were received monthly from the Red Cross Society.

The Indian officers travelled with the British officers to Samara. Here they were separated and marched up to Asia Minor in later echelons.

The Indian officers had the same difficulties to contend with as regards transport as had the British officers. The scale to start with was one donkey per Indian officer. Owing to the disappearance of donkeys *en route* the proportion soon fell to one donkey to four Indian officers.

The Indian officers themselves were separated into two bodies—the Mussulmans and non-Mussulmans. The former were interned at Eski Chehir, and the latter at Konia, where no less than 450 were located.

The main outline of the routine of the latter was the same as that of the British officers. As regards food they had to provide their own, sending down their orderlies to purchase food in the bazaar. Orderlies were allowed at a scale of one per four Indian officers. This continued until the last six months of the war when, food being almost unprocurable in the bazaar, rations were issued on payment by the Turks. Beds and bedding had to be hired, at a rate of £T2½ per month.

Two roll-calls were held in the day, one in the morning about 6 a.m., the other in the evening. The former was a formal one, at which all fell in and the roll-call was taken by a Turkish officer. The latter was informal the senior Indian officer seeing that everyone was present and reporting accordingly to the Turks.

At Konia the Indian officers were distributed among various houses and were accommodated four in a small room. They were allowed to go to the bazaar in parties of three under a " posta " or sentry. It was on these occasions that the only news of the outside world and the war was received. No news was sent them in their letters from India, and the few Indian officers who learnt to read Turkish only found news favourable to the Central Powers in the daily Turkish bulletins. But the Armenians and Greeks in the shops knew what was going on and told the Indian officers when purchasing articles in the bazaar.

As regards parcels, very few were received. Warm clothing was sent by the Red Cross Society and arrived on about three occasions during their captivity. A few Indian officers got money sent from their homes. Letters used to arrive about once a month.

Life must have been dull in the extreme. A few took up the study of languages, and this, with cards and chess, conversation and sleep took up their whole time. Every third day, by way of exercise, the Indian officers were allowed out under guard for a walk. They used to proceed to an open space outside the town, where the younger Indian officers played football.

Although the news of the Armistice was known fairly soon after its signature, yet the Indian officers were still kept under guard. They were eventually put in the train and dispatched to Smyrna. Here they were met by British officers detailed for the purpose, and after a stay of fifteen days embarked for Alexandria. From here they went by rail to Suez, where they were re-fitted with uniform. On arrival in Karachi they were fêted, etc., for one week and then proceeded to the Depot at Montgomery, whence they dispersed on $3\frac{1}{2}$ months' leave. Only one Indian officer of the Regiment died during captivity; this was Jemadar Bhola Singh.

The Mohammedan Indian officers were interned at Eski Chehir. They lived under the same general conditions as described above, but had considerably more freedom, doubtless with a view to influencing their political and religious attitude. These Indian officers were free to go about the town as they liked and without any escort; but they had to be in their rooms by 10 p.m. each night. The Mohammedan Indian officers as a whole committed themselves to one act which was open to misconstruction. This was when they accepted an offer to visit Constantinople to be presented to the Sultan. They said prayers with the Sultan and were each presented with a sword, which was always worn while in Turkey. The Sultan was the titular religious head of their religion. At the same time he was the secular ruler of a nation with whom they were at war.

The Mohammedan Indian officers, on the conclusion of the Armistice, proceeded to Constantinople and thence to Alexandria, after which they followed the same route to India as the Sikh and Hindu Indian officers.

Indian Other Ranks.

After the arrival of the troops in Shumran Camp it was arranged that one officer per battalion (either the Second-in-Command or the Adjutant) should remain with the men throughout their captivity. This arrangement was subsequently cancelled by the Turks. The men accordingly marched off from Shumran about May 7th, 1916. They were, naturally, extremely weak from their privations and physically unfit for continuous marching. Promises of good treatment and short marches were obtained from the Turkish commander, who stated that every consideration possible would be shown to the rank and file prisoners.

Accordingly the British and Indian officers watched their men march off, and were comparatively easy in their minds as to the treatment to be accorded to them. It was not realized at this time that the Turks invariably promised anything and just as invariably failed to carry out the promise, unless forced to. Prior to the departure of the men a medical inspection was held by the Turkish and British medical officers combined to weed out the obviously unfit, in order that these might either be exchanged or sent up-stream by boat. The Turkish medical officers were very obstinate, with the result that only a few men per battalion were passed as unfit. Many men who were not in a fit state to march, therefore, had to start off on their long journey, in many cases to die of weakness and ill-treatment on the way.

The men marched off, each with a very small bundle containing little more than a blanket and perhaps a change of clothes. After a short time almost everything except the blanket was stolen from them. Baghdad was reached in about seven marches, and the prisoners were camped near the railway station on the right bank.

At Baghdad the Sikhs and Hindus were separated from the Mohammedans and thenceforth did not meet again. The Sikhs and Hindus started first from Baghdad after a halt there of about four days in more than one echelon. Owing to the large numbers the railway was used for their transport as far as Samara. From this place the various echelons marched, chiefly by night, to Mosul, where they stayed about three days. The distance was covered in about eleven days. As regards rations, one Turkish loaf per man was issued daily, and a little " dallia." There was no meat or dates.

The treatment of the prisoners by the Arab and Kurdish guards was distinctly better north of Baghdad. This was attributed to Enver Pasha, who came down to visit the Iraq front. Nevertheless the Turkish officers continued to tolerate ill-treatment during the whole journey. Ras-el-Ain was reached in twelve marches from Mosul. The Sikhs and Hindus remained at this place, while the Mohammedans proceeded on by rail to the Amanus Range, and over this range through the Cilician Plain to the foot of the Taurus Mountains. Here they remained for the remainder of their captivity, engaged in making the railway, which was then being constructed through the Taurus.

The routine, etc., of the Mohammedans was much as follows:—They were divided into gangs of about 300 men. The men of one battalion were not necessarily kept together but were spread over several gangs. The men were accommodated first in tents and later in huts. Roughly one-third of the men were very ill at first from fever, stomachic troubles and pneumonia, and from fifteen to thirty died in each gang. All through the first winter, *i.e.*, that of 1916-17, the men had no clothes, except what they had brought with them. After the winter warm clothes arrived through the medium of the Red Cross Society and the American Consul.

At daybreak work started, and continued until dusk with two breaks—one at about 10-30 to 11 a.m. for food, and the second from noon to 1 p.m. In the summer two hours in all were allowed off. A very small rate of pay was issued, consisting of two, three or four mejidieh per month, according to the work performed. This was spent on tobacco, vegetables, etc., obtainable from a small shop. A mejidieh equals twenty piastres, and at the then current rate of exchange was equivalent to about twelve annas. As regards rations the men got one loaf of bread and soup, which latter contained meat every other day. After work was over there were no amusements of any sort for the men. As there were no lights provided the men naturally went to bed very early. There were guards over the men while they were working, but no sentries at night; nor were the men confined within a wired enclosure. Very few letters were received, and no parcels. Some men got two or three letters from their homes during the whole period of their captivity, and many never heard at all.

Work was stopped when the news of the armistice was received. There was then a considerable collection of prisoners of various nationalities. The British, however, were the first to leave, proceeding to Mersina, whence they embarked for Port Said.

The Sikhs and Dogras were worse treated than the Mohammedans. As there were large numbers of the former they marched in several echelons from Samara through Mosul to Ras-el-Ain. The arrangements for the distribution of food were bad. Sometimes none was issued for a day or two, and when issued was unsuitable. Lack of water was very much felt. British soldiers suffered most from this. Any men who fell out for any reason were ill-treated, stripped, and left for dead, or else were beaten with the butts of rifles.

At last the echelons arrived at Ras-el-Ain. In this vicinity the Hindus and Sikhs spent their captivity. They were employed on building the railway towards Nisibin, and the work consisted of making the embankment and breaking and laying stone for the permanent way. The men were divided up into gangs of roughly five non-commissioned officers and one hundred men. Each such gang camped and lived together, at first in black

Arab tents and later in proper tents. Each gang had a Turkish guard of one non-commissioned officer and six to nine soldiers. Gangs were camped at approximately 200 yards distance, and when any gang's particular stretch of railway was completed they were leap-frogged on ahead towards Nisibin. Water was a great difficulty, and often gangs had to go considerable distances to fetch water. The work to begin with was very hard, and there was no time to go and wash. The work hours were from early morning to 12 noon, when a break was allowed for food. Work then continued from 1 p.m. to 6 p.m.

At first the men were under Turks as regards administrative arrangements. After a short time the Germans in charge of the railway took over the administration and issued the rations, etc. The food was just sufficient to keep the men alive, but was not good or really suitable. The men were in receipt of pay. This was mainly a paper transaction, most of it being cut for rations.

The first six months was a very bad time. In this period roughly 25 per cent. of the men died. Disease was rampant, especially typhus. There was an improvement after six months. Sunday was allowed as a day of rest, and disinfectants for clothes were issued. But food was still a difficulty. What pay did come to the men was spent in buying atta from the Arabs, this being stored up as a reserve and eaten when no rations were issued. After about a year various articles began to arrive from India. These included cooking-pots, clothes, ghi, rice, atta, sugar and tea. Captain Puri, I.M.S., who was in medical charge of the prisoners of war, and did very good work throughout, made a dump of everything received from India and issued articles as and when necessary.

As was the case with the Mohammedans, practically no letters or private parcels arrived from India, and many men throughout their captivity never got any news from their homes.

When the Armistice was eventually signed the Sikhs and Hindus were collected at Mersina and thence dispatched to Port Said, and so via Suez to Karachi.

The lot of an " other rank " prisoner of war is always liable to be a hard one. The lot of the unfortunate other ranks in the hands of the Turks was specially hard. There can be no excuse for the death of the large numbers of prisoners in the hands of the Turks. It was due to callousness and a complete failure to realize their responsibilities for their prisoners.

A number of men attempted to escape from the Turks, but, as will have been gathered from the above brief account of the routine of the men, it was very difficult to collect material, suitable clothes, etc. Maps, of course, were non-existent or unprocurable, and the best and shortest way to the British lines could not be worked out before starting.

Sepoys Tehl Singh ("G" Company) (subsequently promoted to Jemadar) and Khushal Singh ("H" Company) were two of the most persistent. In company with four others they started off in clothes made of sacking. This was because they knew that if caught by Arabs all their clothes would be stolen. They started off towards the Euphrates, following nalas which they understood led towards the river. For food parched gram was carried, and a massack to hold their water supply. After about twenty-eight days they were finally caught by Arab herdsmen and sent back to Ras-el-Ain. Their punishment was fifty strokes with a cane. After some three months these two men, with two others, again started off. They made once more for the Euphrates, but after journeying for about one and a half months were caught by "Buddoos" in the neighbourhood of Ramadi. This time their punishment was forty-five strokes. Undeterred, a third attempt was made. This time they were successful, but two of the party of four, including Khushal Singh, died. They were actually caught by "Buddoos" once but released after everything of value had been taken from them. Eventually the survivors got through to the British lines at Ramadi and found themselves in the area occupied by the 39th Garhwalis. Others who escaped included Mangal Singh, a reservist and ex-piper, and Kesar Singh, the signalling havildar. Havildar Bhagwan Singh, after several attempts, was at last shot in trying to get through the Turkish lines.

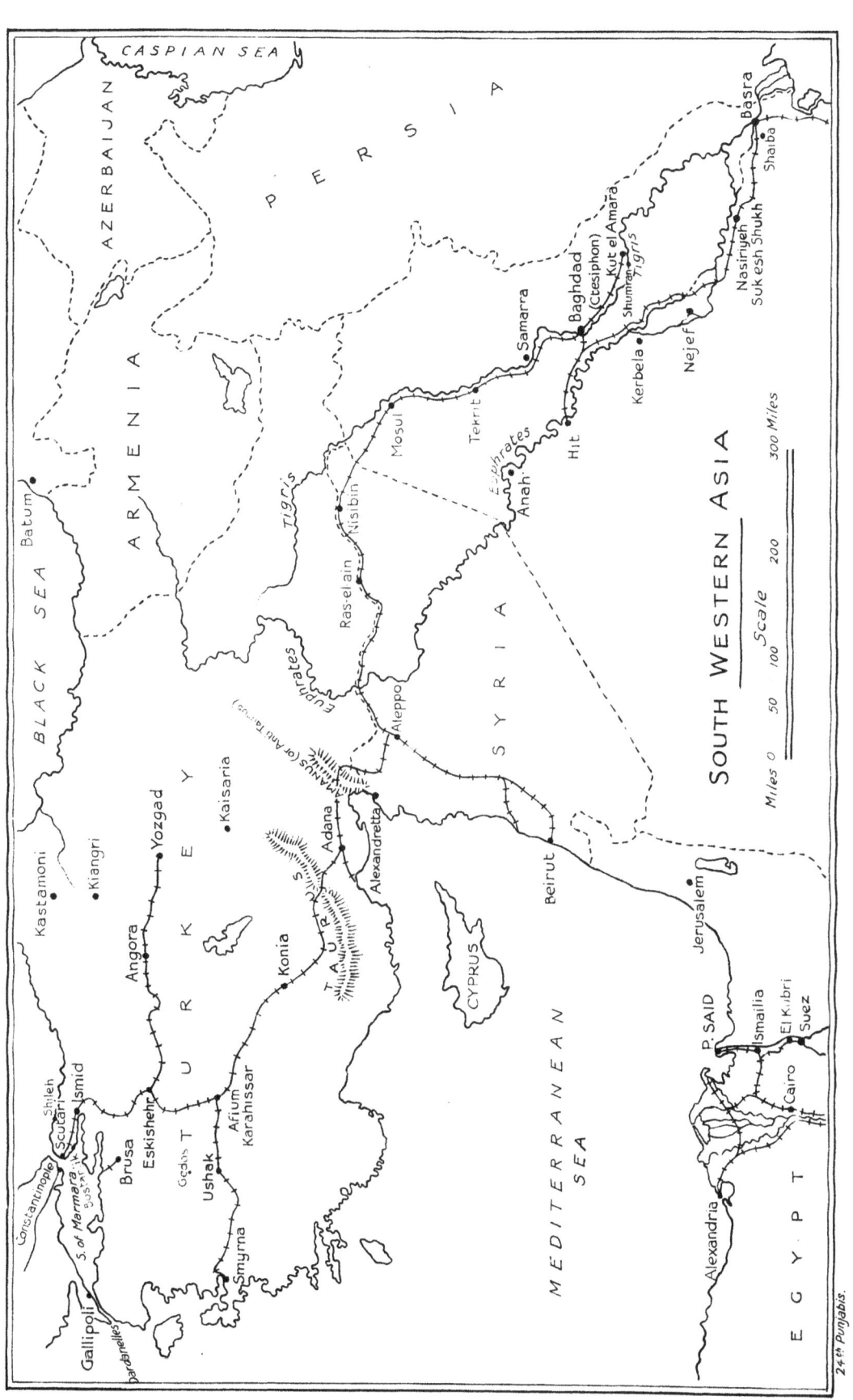

CHAPTER VII.

RE-FORMING THE BATTALION—MESOPOTAMIA, 1917-18—THE BATTLE OF KHAN BAGHDADI—SALONIKA.

ON the departure of the Battalion from Nowshera at the end of October, 1914, the Depot remained at that place for some months. The Depot was commanded by Captain A. C. H. Trevor, with Second-Lieutenant W. H. L. Passy as his assistant. The Depot was moved to Hyderabad Sind in February, 1915, where the Depot of the 22nd Punjabis was already located.

The responsibility for obtaining recruits rested solely with the Depot Commander and recruiting parties from the Depot: and with all units of the Indian Army competing against each other for recruits, it proved very difficult to keep up to strength and impossible to maintain the Battalion on service at full establishment from the resources of the Depot.

Captain Trevor was relieved in command of the Depot by Captain Haig, on the expiration of the latter's sick leave, in July, 1915, and proceeded to join the Battalion.

In August, 1915, there appeared no prospect of getting the Depot up to strength by normal methods, and a further complication had occurred owing to the fact that it was impossible to recruit Afridis, who, at this time, represented one quarter of the composition of the Battalion. All work at the Depot was therefore closed down, and practically the whole establishment, including recruits, was dispatched on recruiting duty. The result of this was that well over one hundred recruits were enlisted in a month. This represented the normal peace recruitment of one year. It was further decided to cease efforts to recruit Afridis and to enlist Yusufzais instead. This arrangement had not official sanction at the time, but the practical result was that the class composition of the Regiment was changed and our connection with the Afridis ceased, except for a short period between 1922 and 1928, when one platoon of Malikdin Khel Afridis was maintained. To start Yusufzai recruiting, a havildar, a naik and a lance-naik were transferred from the 19th Punjabis with the promise of a step in rank and subsequently a draft was transferred from the same battalion.

In October, 1915, Lieutenant H. M. Pim, M.C., relieved Captain Haig at the Depot.

After the beginning of the siege of Kut, no drafts could, of course, be sent to the Regiment, but drafts continued to be dispatched to Mesopotamia. At the time of departure it was normally not known to which units the drafts were to be attached. The majority, however, were sent to the 53rd Sikhs F.F. and served with that battalion during the operations on the Tigris in 1916.

Lieutenant Hobart, after being passed fit for service, was attached to the 53rd and also Lieutenant Passy. Subedar Gul Akbar, having recovered from his wound, also served with the same battalion.

During the operations for the relief of Kut, Lieutenant Passy was killed on March 8th, 1916, and Lieutenant Hobart early in April. Some days before Lieutenant Hobart was killed he displayed great gallantry in endeavouring to bring out of action a wounded officer of the 53rd. For this act he was recommended for the Victoria Cross. During the same period, Subedar Gul Akbar earned the Military Cross.

After the fall of Kut, the Depot continued to function as an ordinary depot until September 24th, 1916. During this period a draft was dispatched to the 2nd/22nd Punjabis, then in process of being formed at Basra. On September 25th the 24th were re-formed from the Depot at Hyderabad Sind, at first under command of Captain Pim. The latter was relieved by Lieut.-Colonel Malcolm, of the 31st Punjabis, on October 30th.

The 24th were ordered to Jubbulpore in the middle of December, 1916, and Bt. Lieut.-Colonel J. L. Furney, 22nd Punjabis, took over command in February, 1917. Lieut.-Colonel Furney was given his brevet while with the 22nd at the Battle of Ctesiphon and was destined to command the 24th for the remainder of the war till the beginning of 1919. Training continued steadily, and the Battalion was said to be about the best of the various new units being formed.

At length, in March, 1917, orders were received to proceed again to Mesopotamia. The Battalion entrained at Jubbulpore for Bombay on April 5th and 6th, and on the 7th embarked on the H.T. *Ellenga*. Basra was reached on April 15th; and after disembarkation the Battalion was, in the first instance, encamped at Magil. On the 17th, the posts in Nos. 1 and 2 Sections of the Euphrates defences were taken over. These sections guarded the railway Basra—Shaiba—Nasiriya.

Five Indian officers and 199 Indian other ranks were in the Zobeir area; four British officers, eight Indian officers, and 440 Indian other ranks under Major F. A. Magniac (22nd Punjabis) took over the posts of No. 2 Section up to Ghabisiya. Lieut.-Colonel Furney was in command of No. 1 Section, having his headquarters and one company in the Serai in Basra city.

For the remainder of April and during the whole of May, there was no change in the dispositions: the time being spent in training, musketry and ordinary routine duties.

On June 15th the Battalion concentrated at Magil preparatory to moving up to the Tigris front. On June 19th, Headquarters and 450 of all ranks embarked in the river steamers P.S.4 and P.S.61, and started up-river; the remainder embarked the next day. Between June 27th and July 1st the Battalion concentrated at Baghdad, and a few days later, between July 4th and 7th, left for the Euphrates to relieve the 27th Punjabis. Battalion Headquarters were located at the Hindiya Barrage, with posts at Nukhta and Mufraz. The weather at this time was very hot, varied by frequent dust-storms: in consequence, the marches to the Hindiya Barrage were made by night.

In July, Captain Conder, attached from the 19th Punjabis, died of heat-stroke in Baghdad.

The Regiment now formed part of the 3rd Division. The month of August was spent in training, musketry and normal routine duties, as was September. On the 9th of the latter month a detachment of 75 rifles was sent to the Holy City of Kerbela. The climate was now improving, the days being bright and fine, and the nights cool. A draft arrived from India on September 30th.

On October 3rd, a fine piece of salvage work was carried out by the Mufraz detachment. By some means, a mahela, on which were loaded 800 tins of petrol, caught on fire. The detachment set to work to carry the tins away from the burning boat, naturally a very dangerous undertaking. In the end, 600 out of the 800 tins were salved. One tin actually burst in a man's hands when being carried ashore. It was a gallant piece of work and four men were specially mentioned for their conduct.

October and November were again spent in training, musketry, etc. In the last week of November, drafts amounting to three Indian officers and 227 Indian other ranks arrived, all except thirty-nine other ranks coming from the 20th Punjabis or their Depot. It will be noted that only one draft had arrived before this date: this shows the great wastage that must be expected in a bad climate, even when no active operations are in progress. The weather was now very much better, being fine, cold and bright.

During December, 1917, the Headquarters of the Battalion were moved to Musaiyib, on relief by the 45th Sikhs.

On January 10th, 1918, a mixed force under the command of Lieut.-Colonel Furney, undertook a raid against the village and fort of Obed Dahash. The Battalion, less its detachments, took part in this raid. It was the usual type of raid to punish troublesome Arabs. A night march was made, and a cordon put round the objective before dawn. The village and fort were successfully taken by 0845 hours. There was no opposition: the village was burnt and the fort destroyed, one wall of the fort being dug down by men of the Battalion. In the course of the raid, a large number of sheep were captured. The force arrived back at Musaiyib at 1645 hours.

The success of the operation depended on surprise and the possibility of reaching the objective quickly. Numerous irrigation channels had to be crossed and the successful result of the raid was largely due to the previous preparation of bridges. Each bridge had to be made of the correct dimensions, so that there should be as little delay as possible to the advance of the force.

On January 15th, 1918, detachments having been called in, the Regiment marched back to Baghdad. On the 18th it proceeded to Falluja on the Euphrates, by rail. The Battalion now formed part of an active brigade, the 50th Brigade of the 15th Division. On February 7th the Battalion marched to Dhibban and the following day to Madhij. This latter place was held by a detachment of The Oxfordshire and Buckinghamshire Light Infantry, who were relieved by " C " Company of the 24th Punjabis. Madhij was near Ramadi, where the 15th Division had scored a notable victory in the previous September: and the moves now in progress were a prelude to the successful operations ending in the Battle of Khan Baghdadi.

The beginning of February was spent in training. One week's battalion training was carried out, followed by one day's brigade training. Special attention was given to night exercises. This training was the first systematic training which it had been possible to carry out since the Battalion arrived in Mesopotamia in April, 1917.

On February 21st, three companies at service strength marched to Ramadi; on the following day Khan Abu Rayan was reached. Here " C " Company rejoined, on the 23rd, from Madhij. On February 24th, the whole Battalion marched to Okbah and took over the outposts from the 1st/5th Gurkha Rifles, who, at this time, formed part of the 50th Brigade. Three companies, each supplying three piquets, were on outpost; one company being in reserve. The Battalion held the outposts till March 4th, 1918. On February 27th the Divisional Commander, Major-General Sir H. T. Brooking, visited the outposts. The 50th Brigade, at this time, consisted of the 1st Bn. The Oxfordshire and Buckinghamshire Light Infantry, the 24th Punjabis, 97th Infantry, and 1st/5th Gurkha Rifles.

On March 4th the Battalion was relieved from the outposts by the 97th Infantry. On the 8th the whole Brigade marched by night towards Hit. The Turkish position which had been constructed here was found to be unoccupied. When it was light, the Battalion advanced on the right of the Brigade; " C " Company moved through the town of Hit, and so were the first British troops to enter the town.

On March 11th the Battalion marched with the remainder of the Brigade to Sahiliya, arriving at 1200 hours. This village was about twelve miles short of the town of Khan Baghdadi. On the 12th the 24th found three piquets for the outposts. March 16th to 21st was spent in digging a position at Sahiliya, and working parties were also detailed to improve the roads and communications generally. On the evening of March 25th the Khan Baghdadi operations began.

BATTLE OF KHAN BAGHDADI.

This battle took place on March 26th, 1918. The British force consisted of the 42nd and 50th Brigades of the 15th Division, with the addition of the 11th Cavalry Brigade (Brigadier-General R. A. Cassells) and attached artillery. The Turkish force was estimated at 170 sabres, 2,800 rifles, 38 machine guns, and from 12 to 15 guns. The general plan of the battle was that the infantry should attack and pin the Turks to their positions, and thus give time for Cassells' Cavalry Brigade to make a wide turning movement round the western flank and cut off the retreat of the Turks northwards. For this purpose, the British force under the command of Major-General H. T. Brooking of the 15th Division was organized in three main groups:—

Cassells' Brigade, Lucas' Group (42nd Brigade group), and Andrews' Group (50th Brigade group).

Andrews' Group consisted of the 50th Brigade (now composed of The Oxfordshire and Buckinghamshire Light Infantry, 6th Jat Light Infantry, 24th Punjabis and the 97th Infantry), 10th Lancers, 48th Pioneers, 215th Brigade, R.F.A., 450th Field Company, R.E., and a double-horsed battery of the 222nd Brigade, R.F.A.

The Turkish position consisted of a forward position south of Khan Baghdadi and a northern position north of the village, the distance between the two positions being approximately two miles.

Andrews' Group moved off from Sahiliya at 2100 hours on March 25th, the 6th Jat Light Infantry leading, followed by The Oxfordshire and Buckinghamshire Light Infantry, 24th Punjabis and the 97th Infantry. At 0115 hours on March 26th, the column halted, and orders were issued for three companies (one each from the 6th Jat Light Infantry, Oxfordshire and Buckinghamshire Light Infantry and the 24th Punjabis, in that order from right to left) to attack the first Turkish position and rush it without cheering or firing. The orders were issued very hurriedly. As the Battalion was the third in order of march there was necessarily some little delay before the company detailed arrived at the head of the column. Consequently there was no time to issue complete orders to the company. In actual fact, Lieut.-Colonel Furney had to walk some distance with the company, explaining the plan of action as he went, and there was no time to explain to the men exactly what was required. No officer was detailed to command the three companies, and with regard to direction it was ordered that the company of The Oxfordshire and Buckinghamshire Light Infantry (the centre one) was to direct, but no officer was detailed to guide them.

The attack was ordered on the assumption that the position was lightly held. The 24th Punjabis' company, " A " Company, under Captain A. P. Algar, I.A.R.O., advanced in two lines, extended at three paces interval.

The three companies advanced for one and a half miles and were then fired on at short range by guns, machine guns and rifles. Little opposition was encountered from the first line, but the main fire came from trenches situated somewhat farther to the rear. In spite of there being a little confusion and intermingling of units, the companies charged and captured two lines of trenches immediately hostile fire was opened, but were held up in front of the third line by machine-gun fire, which completely enfiladed the companies. Captain Algar and four Sikh sepoys, however, penetrated into the third line, where they were all killed. The attack was thus brought to a standstill in the dark. Orders were then sent up for the companies to retire. This was done in good order, the 24th Punjabis' company arriving back at 0430 hours.

In this attack, Captain Algar was killed and Jemadar Karam Ilahi dangerously wounded. Both these officers had displayed marked gallantry and both were recommended for immediate awards, Captain Algar being recommended for the Victoria Cross.

During this first attack the remainder of the Group was under cover of some hills south-west of the Aleppo Road, and the Turks shelled this neighbourhood until the second attack started.

At 1015 hours orders were received that Andrews' Group were to attack the position on the south (left) of the road, Lucas' Group co-operating on the north of the road. The 24th Punjabis were on the right of the Brigade, 97th Infantry on the left, Oxfordshire and Buckinghamshire Light Infantry in support. The 6th Jat Light Infantry moved on the extreme left. Meanwhile the enemy had been evacuating his forward position: nevertheless, considerable shell fire was encountered.

The advance, however, proceeded slowly but steadily, resulting in the capture of the Turks' advanced position, till about 1230 hours, when the advance was held up about one and a half miles from the main position. During this phase of the battle, the total prisoners captured by the Brigade was 100, of which the Battalion share was 16.

A halt ensued until 1730 hours. During this wait, the artillery moved forward and registered in preparation for the next attack. The 42nd Brigade, meanwhile, had got rather in rear of the 50th Brigade. At 1730 hours the final attack began. By this time, Cassells' cavalry had got round and behind the Turks. The 24th Punjabis were leading on the right of the 50th Brigade, The Oxfordshire and Buckinghamshire Light Infantry and 6th Jat Light Infantry continuing the line to the left; the 97th Infantry were in support. On the right of the 24th Punjabis was a battalion of the 42nd Brigade. Each battalion was on a front of 300 yards. The arrangements for artillery support were slow fire for fifteen minutes and then fifteen minutes' intense barrage. The 256th Machine Gun Company gave support by overhead fire at ranges of 1,500 to 2,000 yards. At about 1800 hours the position was captured, the Brigade between them making

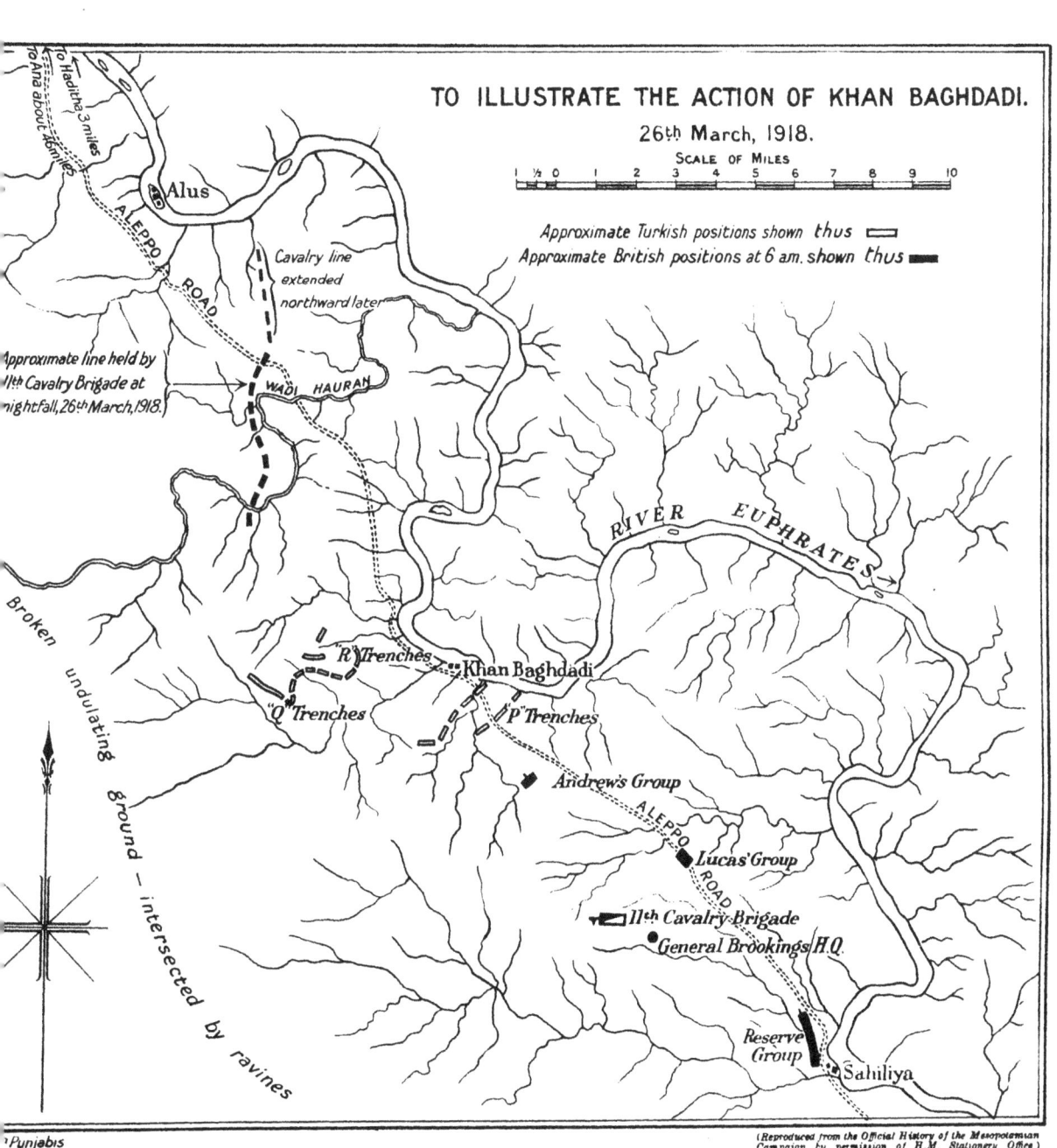

prisoners of the whole of the 169th Turkish Infantry Regiment, plus guns and machine guns. The 24th Punjabis captured 40 prisoners and 3 machine guns.

At this point some confusion arose from two battalions of the 42nd Brigade crossing the front. As soon as one of these battalions was clear, the advance was continued, and a further 90 prisoners (including five officers) and a certain amount of transport were captured. After moving forward for some distance, the Battalion was halted.

By this time it was dark. The other forward battalions, having reached what they thought were their final objectives, were by this time a good deal in rear: and thus the Battalion was somewhat isolated. Unavailing endeavours were then made to get in touch with Group Headquarters with a Lucas lamp. Meanwhile patrols were sent forward, piquets were posted and the Battalion bivouacked. After this had been done communication was eventually established with Group Headquarters. About midnight a Territorial battalion of The Queen's Own Royal West Kent Regiment, which had been brought up in Ford vans, passed through the 24th and established a line of outposts on the piquet line. The 24th's piquets were then withdrawn.

At 0315 hours on March 27th orders were received to continue the advance along the Aleppo Road in column of route. At 0400 hours the Battalion joined up with the remainder of the Brigade and marched in a northerly direction. When near Jubbah Village, an L.A.M. car reported that the Turkish force had surrendered.

After moving forward for two miles, the Turks were seen with the white flag flying, and, in the distance, Cassells' Cavalry Brigade was visible. Operations then ceased, and the Brigade bivouacked in the Hauran Nullah.

The casualties in the 24th Punjabis were:—

Captain Algar killed.
Jemadar Karam Ilahi dangerously wounded.
Indian Other Ranks.—Killed, 5; wounded, 25.
Missing, believed killed: 1.
Missing: 7.
Total casualties: 40.

Jemadar Karam Ilahi was awarded the I.O.M., 2nd Class.

The result of the Battle of Khan Baghdadi was the capture of practically the entire Turkish force on the Euphrates. Before the operations, General Brooking issued an Order of the Day asking the troops to " march hard and hit hard." An Order of the day issued on March 27th was as follows:

"I asked you to 'march hard and hit hard.' You have done so: and your efforts have produced the following :—

"About 3,000 prisoners, including 200 officers; 10 guns, many machine guns, 2,000 rifles, large quantities of ammunition, and 600 animals, besides a large number of field kitchens, transport vehicles and other war material.

"My thanks to you for your fine response to the call made on you."

The above number of prisoners was an under-estimate. The actual captures were nearly 5,000 prisoners. Huge quantities of ammunition were also captured. The Anah S.A.A. dump contained three and three-quarter million rounds, and there was an equal quantity at Haditha.

March 28th and 29th were spent in clearing the battlefield. Captain Algar's body was found. On the 30th the Battalion (less "A" Company) returned to Khan Baghdadi. While passing over the battlefield of Khan Baghdadi, the opportunity was taken to parade the Battalion round the graves of Captain Algar and those who were killed with him and of paying the last honours to their gallant comrades. On April 1st the Battalion marched back to Sahiliya.

On the return of the force to Sahiliya work was commenced on defensive positions, the construction of which occupied the Battalion throughout the hot weather. Opportunities for training were very limited, only one company being able to carry out company training.

In April orders were received to dispatch one company to help form the newly constituted 1st/152nd Infantry, later called the 1st/152nd Punjabis. "D" Company was selected and the following officers in consequence left the Battalion in May :—

Lieutenant (Acting Captain) C. L. Sevenoaks, Lieutenant A. I. Aymer, Subedars Ghulam Mahomed and Bahadur Singh, and Jemadars Feroze Khan and Bhagat Singh.

This company took part in the Battle of Sharon in Palestine in September, 1918, when Lieutenant Aymer and some Indian other ranks were killed. Captain Sevenoaks was awarded the Military Cross and Naik Rajwali the I.D.S.M.

As the result of the losses sustained at Khan Baghdadi and the departure of "D" Company, the Battalion became much under strength, necessitating large drafts from the Depot in India. These drafts, owing to the hurried training they had received and the lack of sufficient competent instructors at the Depot, were considerably below the required standard. Owing to the then general shortage of Sikhs throughout the Army, it was not found possible to raise two platoons of this class in the new company, which was therefore composed of three platoons of Punjabi Mussulmans and one of Dogras, and was named "E" Company.

Meanwhile the Depot, though seriously handicapped by lack of British officers conversant with Urdu, and of sufficient competent instructors, was enlisting vigorously, being particularly successful in obtaining Punjabi Mussulmans and, to a lesser degree, Dogras.

Captain (Acting Major) R. B. Deedes, M.C., was relieved in April by Captain C. M. Thornhill, D.S.O., M.C., and soon after various officers arrived for duty for short or long periods. Lieutenant V. G. L. Prideaux, who had arrived in November, 1917, assumed the duties of Adjutant until he left in May. Second-Lieutenant T. A. Dobney acted as Quartermaster. Other officers were Lieutenant F. N. Hill, Lieutenant A. P. Cunningham, M.C., and Second-Lieutenant C. E. Penny, besides others whose attachments were purely temporary.

In May the Depot was called upon to furnish a draft to assist in forming the Depot of the 1st/152nd Punjabis at Ahmednagar, Subedar Hashim Ali being detailed to accompany it. This Indian officer afterwards became Subedar-Major of his new battalion.

About this time the Depot was ordered to raise a company of Sind Mussulmans, but the men deserted almost as fast as they were enlisted, and the scheme was abandoned immediately after the Armistice.

At the beginning of September the 24th were selected by the Brigade Commander to proceed to an " unknown destination," one battalion from each brigade in Mesopotamia being dispatched for that purpose. It was generally known in the force that the battalions selected were considered the best in their respective brigades. The destination proved to be Salonika. The Regiment started down the line on September 8th and marched via Hit, Khan Abu Rayan, Ramadi (where it halted for about ten days), Madhij (where it separated into two wings moving on successive days) to Dhibban, the railhead. The wings were united again at Hinaidi just below Baghdad, whence the Battalion proceeded by train and boat to Basra. On arrival there at the end of September, " Spanish influenza " broke out in the Regiment, resulting in some fifteen deaths, whilst twenty-five ranks, including Second-Lieutenant J. C. Cotton, were invalided to India. A further decrease in strength was caused by orders received for the formation in India of a second battalion (the 2nd/24th Punjabis never actually materialized, as it was still in the process of formation when the Armistice was declared), resulting in Subedar Fateh Singh, I.O.M., Jemadar Kehr Singh and various other ranks being left at Basra for dispatch to the second battalion in India. Captain C. F. Scroope joined the Battalion at Basra from commanding No. 3 Indian Base Depot. Some fifty transport drivers were also transferred from various corps to provide the personnel of the Battalion transport allotted under the war establishments prevailing at Salonika. These drivers included Madrasis, Biharis, Bombay Gujratis, a Christian and two or three sweepers.

The Battalion left Basra in the H.T. *Kashgar* on October 4th and disembarked at Salonika on October 25th. It was at once equipped according to the scales existing in the British Salonika Force. G.S. limbers were allotted as part of its permanent transport for the first time in the history of the Battalion; steel helmets and gas-masks were issued, and the 1914 leather equipment substituted for the bandolier equipment. At the same time, seven British officers and some twenty British sergeants were attached to provide a reserve of officers and to help in acclimatizing the Battalion to the new conditions of warfare. As far as the Regiment was concerned, this scheme was not a success and the majority of the sergeants were withdrawn before three months expired, only one staying with the Battalion for over a year. As rapidly as possible, preparations were made to enable the Battalion to join the 22nd Division in an attack on Adrianople. Bulgaria was now out of the war and the Turkish western frontier was consequently open to attack.

On October 31st the Battalion marched to "General's Corner" (fourteen miles from the camp near Doudoula, west of Salonika), but the next day its forward march was cancelled, in the first instance owing to flooded camping grounds and subsequently owing to the pending Armistice with the Turks. The Battalion remained three months at "General's Corner," and opportunity was used to carry on training.

The Depot was moved to Montgomery at the end of 1918, arriving there on Christmas Day. It had stopped recruiting on the conclusion of the Armistice: 1,340 recruits had been obtained during the year up to that date. It was now engaged in receiving back the survivors of the siege of Kut, who numbered only 273 out of 450 ranks captured.

Before recording the history of the 24th in the period succeeding the Armistice up to the time of its return to India, it may be of interest to show how of the regular officers borne on the rolls of the Regiment at the outbreak of war in 1914 not one remained with the Battalion from the beginning of 1918, and only one (the latest-joined) after the fall of Kut.

Appendix "A" gives a list of the officers of the 24th at the outbreak of war, totalling 19. Of these, nine were killed and one (Lieutenant C. C. Langhorne) permanently disabled from wounds. Two (Lieut.-Colonels Climo and Skeen) ceased to be borne on the rolls on promotion to Colonel and subsequently, in June, 1918, to Major-General. Three were prisoners of war as the result of the capture of the Kut garrison. Captain Wilson was transferred to Skinner's Horse early in 1915. Major Rawlins commanded the Bikanir Camel Corps for the whole of the war. Captain Thornhill served with the 129th Baluchis and on the Staff till his return to the Depot and so never served with the Battalion on service. Captain Pim at the end of 1917 was appointed to the G.H.Q. Staff in Mesopotamia.

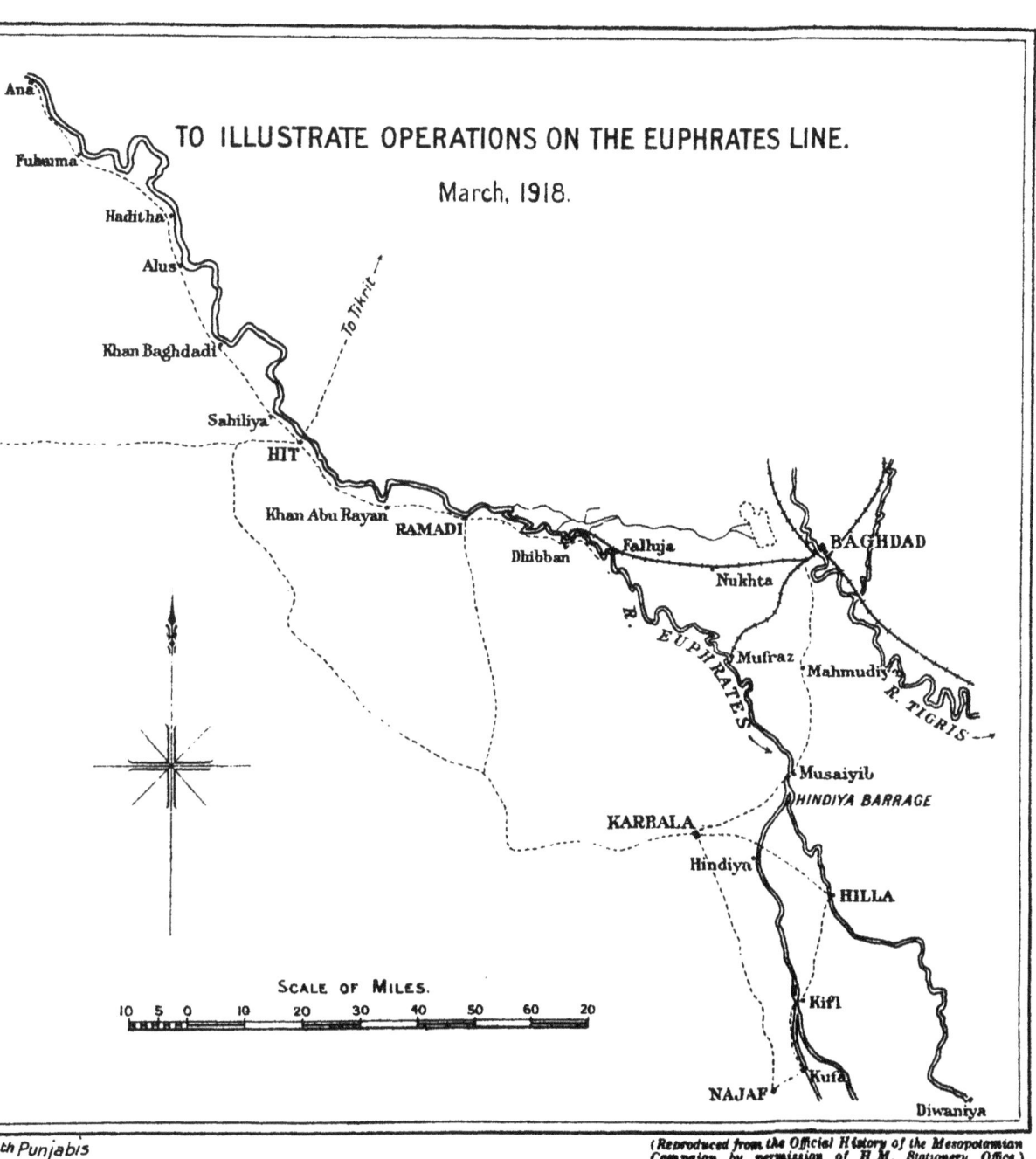

CHAPTER VIII.

THE BLACK SEA AND TURKEY—RETURN TO INDIA.

See Map of South-Western Asia, facing page 58.

APPENDIX " J " shows the British and Indian officers serving with the Regiment in the field on January 1st, 1919. The class composition is also given and is of interest as showing the difference from that of 1914. The Sikhs had decreased by the equivalent of one pre-war company: Pathans had decreased by half and were Yusafzais instead of Afridis. Dogras and Punjabi Mussulmans had increased, the main increase being in the latter class, whose numbers had been raised to more than double the pre-war proportion.

In the middle of January, 1919, the Battalion was ordered to Batum on the Black Sea, embarking on January 30th in H.T. *Katoomba* during a snowstorm. Meanwhile the demobilization of British officers had commenced and Captains K. McI. Kemp and C. H. K. Phillips and Lieutenant C. Page were demobilized before the Battalion left Salonika. The Regiment reached Batum on February 4th, disembarked the following day and was billeted in the Russian barracks some three miles out of the town. Within a week the Battalion was finding numerous guards in the vicinity of Batum, the most distant being some six miles out. Detachments were dispatched to various villages inland, one British officer and one platoon at Kedi, two sections at Hichi-Houra, and one British officer with one platoon at Houla, all on the Batum—Tiflis Road. The latter post was about fifty miles away. Subsequently posts were found of two sections at Borcha, one British officer and one platoon at Artvin, and two sections at Ardantoch, all on the main road to Kars, the latter post being some eighty miles from Batum.

Owing to the opening up of leave to Indian ranks, the extreme prevalence of malaria, and finally to an outbreak of mumps, duties became increasingly heavy. The nights in bed rarely rose above two, and for weeks on end were below one, so that the health and training of the Battalion reached a low ebb.

In July the 27th Divisional Athletic Meeting was held, in which the Regiment gained three first places. Subsequently, in the Army of the Black Sea Championships, the Battalion secured one first, one second (relay race), and a few other placings.

It is of interest to note that permission was granted for parties of Mohammedan troops to visit Mecca. Accordingly on August 5th Jemadar Askar Khan and a party of seventeen Indian other ranks left for Mecca, returning on October 22nd.

In September the Battalion was ordered to Anatolia, the G.O.C. 80th Brigade inspecting it, and issuing a complimentary order prior to its departure. The Battalion embarked on September 12th and arrived a few days later at Bostanjik, a village on the coast of the Sea of Marmora, opposite Prinkipo Island, where it formed part of the 84th Brigade of the 28th Division.

By this time Major G. W. Atkins, M.C., had left the Battalion to take up the command of the 10th Jats, and Lieutenants C. Gault and J. W. F. Young had joined from India. Duties at Bostanjik were less heavy and the climate more favourable, so that the health of the Battalion steadily improved, as did the standard of training, though this was still considerably short of the pre-war standard. Lieutenant A. P. Cunningham preceded a draft from India and joined the Battalion in December.

On December 19th, Bt. Colonel H. A. V. Cummins, C.M.G., returned from leave granted after his release from captivity, and assumed permanent command of the Battalion, being the first permanent commandant since Major-General S. H. Climo, C.B., D.S.O., had relinquished command three years previously.

The Depot suffered a severe loss in June at Montgomery in the death from heat-stroke of Captain (Acting Major) C. M. Thornhill, D.S.O., M.C. The command devolved on several officers in rapid succession, and the work of the Depot suffered by this lack of continuity. Once the difficulties caused by the Punjab disturbances in April (when the Depot was called upon to furnish a detachment at Raewind) and the succeeding Afghan War were surmounted, demobilization proceeded fairly rapidly and the Depot, though still large, assumed more manageable proportions. Several British officers joined the Depot, but with the exception of Lieutenant J. Exshaw, who reported his arrival in April, these were temporary officers and were soon demobilized. Eighty-three Indian ranks were enrolled during the year and 843 discharged under the various demobilization schemes then in force. It was a source of gratification to the Battalion that the important and difficult operations carried out in Waziristan this year were conducted by Major-General S. H. Climo, in chief command, whilst Major-General A. Skeen commanded the fighting column.

Bitterly cold weather was experienced in January, 1920, in Anatolia and the Black Sea area, and an outbreak of influenza caused some deaths. Although on the surface political conditions appeared quiet, a steady deterioration was setting in as regards the " Nationalist " or Angora Turks, and by May the conditions were distinctly bad. The farthermost British post held in Anatolia at this time was Ismid, sixty miles from Bostanjik, the more distant posts at Afion Karahissar and Eski Chehir having been withdrawn under pressure from the Nationalists. Ismid was garrisoned by the 242nd Brigade under Brigadier-General Montague Bates,

C.B., C.M.G., D.S.O., and of this brigade the 25th Punjabis, with administrative details, was stationed at Derinje, eight miles west of Ismid.

On May 19th the Battalion arrived at Derinje in relief of the 25th Punjabis, taking over various detached posts on the railway between Derinje and Guebze (fifteen miles from Bostanjik), where duties were exceedingly heavy. These detachments were withdrawn early in June, 1920, but on June 11th " C " Company, under the command of Captain Troughton Dean, left Derinje to relieve a company of the 10th Jats, which held a detached post, known as Point 325, situated on the military road that runs through the Ismid Peninsula to Constantinople and some two miles north of the town of Ismid. The company included a number of draft men recently arrived from India, and Subedar Suba Ram was the only Indian officer present. On June 13th Subedar Kehr Singh joined the company with a convoy from Derinje. At this time the Turkish Nationalists, or followers of Mustapha Kemal Pasha, were advancing towards Ismid, where the main force of the Constantinople, or Anti-Nationalist, Army was encamped. As it was the intention of the Kemalists to march on Scutari, trouble between the two forces was imminent, and Lieutenant Maddox, R.E., was sent to Point 325 as Intelligence Officer. It was now decided that the Anti-Nationalist Army, much embarrassed by desertions, should fall back at once to the Bosphorus, moving by the military road past Point 325. An engagement outside the defences of Ismid, with the risk of involving the British, who had not yet come into conflict with the Kemalists, would thus be avoided. After some delay, the Anti-Nationalist Army eventually marched on the morning of June 14th, but had only proceeded a few miles on their way when gun fire was opened on them from the north and north-east. This clearly indicated that the Kemalists were already in command of the road leading to the Bosphorus. The Anti-Nationalist left flank guard, consisting of a battalion and one gun, had now reached a position about half a mile from Point 325, and from there returned the fire. After desultory gun fire and a few casualties had occurred the Anti-Nationalists lost heart and returned to Ismid, where they were immediately embarked for Constantinople by the British. The flank guard, after being refused protection at Point 325, followed suit, although it was noticed that large numbers remained behind to join up with the advancing Kemalists. At 1300 hours the Kemalists advanced from the north in regular extended lines, and only came to a halt outside the perimeter wire of Point 325. A Turkish officer, accompanied by a mounted orderly, now advanced, the orderly carrying a large green standard, presumably to emphasize the religious character of the rising. After expressing great friendship for the British, the officer asked permission to march his force through the post, and, on being informed that the orders of the G.O.C. did not permit of this, but that he could pass outside and 600 yards from the perimeter, he appeared surprised and annoyed, but eventually consented to this arrangement.

From this time the Kemalist Turks continued to move in small parties towards Ismid, passing both to the east and west of Point 325. At 1600 hours it was noticed that the telephone line had been cut and that the post was completely surrounded. This was an unpleasant alteration from the morning situation, when the garrison had enjoyed themselves as spectators of the half-hearted engagement that had taken place between the contending Turkish forces. A strong Turkish piquet was now established about 200 yards distant from the perimeter and commanding the road to Ismid, and the Turks became openly hostile and abusive of the British. The Intelligence Officer, who went out to ascertain their intentions, was detained and threatened. Again a Turkish officer approached and demanded the evacuation of the post to avoid bloodshed, stating that the men under his command were fanatical and could not be controlled. He also advised a message being sent to the G.O.C. at Ismid, warning him to evacuate that place, as it would be attacked during the night. On meeting with a refusal, he departed saying that no one would now be permitted to leave the post.

Strict orders had been received that no firing was to take place unless the Turks actually fired into, or advanced on, the post. As these conditions were observed by the Turks, there was nothing to be done but to improve the trenches and await events. After dark, Lance-Naik Devi Singh did useful work and satisfactory lamp communication was established with Ismid. Throughout the night hourly situation reports were signalled. All ranks remained on the perimeter, but the night passed quietly until 0400 hours on June 15th, when heavy rifle and machine-gun fire broke out in the direction of Ismid. Once again the garrison were silent spectators, and were not permitted to take part, although parties of the Kemalists moving to and fro offered the most tempting targets. Shots from the defenders of the Ismid perimeter continuously passed over the post. Firing ceased at 0700 hours, the attack having failed, and many wounded Kemalists were carried past Point 325 from the direction of Ismid.

The G.O.C. was now informed that two guns had been placed on a hill about half a mile from the post, and that rations and water were available for the 16th.

At 1345 hours the situation was cleared up by the arrival of an aeroplane which dropped orders for the evacuation of Point 325. The garrison was to retire on Ismid at 1700 hours that day (June 15th) by the shortest route. Tents were struck and dumped in a hollow. Kits, stores, rations and bombs were added, with bhusa and kerosene oil to ensure a good conflagration, and Lance-Naiks Sham Singh and Bahadur Singh were detailed for the somewhat exciting duty of firing the dump when the order should be given. At 1645 hours the perimeter was evacuated; the detachment collected in a hollow outside the wire and hidden from the enemy road piquet. The dump was successfully fired and the explosions that followed no doubt discouraged the Kemalists from looting.

The detachment now marched in three parties. The advanced guard consisted of a Sikh platoon commanded by Havildar Harnam Singh. The two Dogra platoons and the transport formed the main body under Subedar Suba Ram. The remaining Sikh platoon, under Subedar Kehr Singh, was left with its Lewis guns in position at the post with orders to open fire on the Kemalists should they dispute the passage of the detachment. Captain Dean and the Intelligence Officer moved with the advanced platoon. As soon as this platoon arrived below the enemy piquet, the Kemalists appeared in large numbers on a ridge of high ground running parallel and close to the road, and, by excited gesticulations and threats, signalled the leading men back to Point 325. The advanced platoon now rushed forward at the double, whereupon a whistle sounded and the enemy opened fire at close range, which fire was taken up by machine guns from several directions. Stampeded by the noise of the firing, the mules broke away and returned to the post. The enemy swarmed down on to the road and engaged in hand-to-hand fighting with the main body. Lieutenant Maddox and Company Havildar-Major Kesar Singh were both shot down at point-blank range. Owing to the confusion of friend and foe, Subedar Kehr Singh's Lewis guns were unable to render any assistance. Heavy casualties had occurred at the first burst of fire, and further casualties were only avoided by Subedar Suba Ram ordering his men into a deep nullah. The advanced platoon had now become scattered, and of eight men who had taken up a position on the road with a Lewis gun, four had been hit and the gun had jammed after firing two short bursts. As the enemy were firing at very close range, the withdrawal was ordered to continue. The company was undoubtedly saved from being annihilated by the inaccurate fire of the Turks and the broken nature of the country which enabled the detachment to find its way to the Ismid perimeter in small parties and without further loss. When the detachment was collected inside the Ismid defences it was found that about 25 per cent. had become casualties, and, owing to the impossibility of moving the badly wounded, who were not spared by the Turks, the proportion of killed to wounded was heavy. The men had behaved very well throughout under the most difficult circumstances. Generals Crocker, Commanding the 28th Division, and Montague Bates, Commanding the 242nd Brigade, expressed their congratulations and relief at the detachment having got through with comparatively light loss.

The following casualties were sustained:—

Killed.—Lieutenant Maddox, R.E., a Greek interpreter, a Sub-Assistant Surgeon, and 18 Indian other ranks.

Wounded.—16 Indian other ranks.

Captain Dean was awarded the Military Cross, Subedar Suba Ram the I.D.S.M., and several Indian other ranks either the I.O.M. or I.D.S.M.

From the above narrative it will have been noticed that the detachment was ordered to withdraw at a specified hour in daylight. In view of the known attitude and temper of the Kemalist Turks, the order would have been open to criticism had no arrangements to support the detachment been made. In actual fact, orders for the support of the withdrawal were issued, but the battalion detailed for this duty was late and therefore did not support or cover, in any way, the retiring detachment.

On June 29th Derinje was evacuated and the Battalion was moved by sea to Beikos on the Asiatic side of the Bosphorus. On July 5th the Italian armed police, who were responsible for the defences of the town, allowed the Nationalists through. As a result, the Battalion was sniped in the early morning, and a working party which was marching through the town was fired on. Jemadar Muzaffar Hussain, a direct commissioned officer recently arrived from India, and one sepoy were killed, and five other ranks wounded.

On the night of July 7th more sniping occurred and one sepoy was wounded. Various reconnaissances were carried out in the neighbourhood, but without success, as no enemy were encountered. On one occasion the Battalion co-operated with the Archipelago Regiment of the Greek Army in an attempt to surprise and capture Nationalists in the village of Arnaut Keui, where several Christians had been massacred.

On July 27th the Battalion, less "A" and "B" Companies, which moved by land, embarked in H.T. *Kapurthala* for Shileh, a small town on the Black Sea coast, and arrived there on the following morning. "A" and "B" Companies joined up after four days' marching, having travelled sixty miles by land. Three Yusafzai sepoys who had deserted just previous to the Battalion leaving Beikos, were recaptured at Shileh, and were sentenced in due course by court-martial.

On August 19th the Battalion, less the right wing, marched to Beikos, arriving on the 22nd, the right wing following from Shileh a fortnight later. The work at Beikos continued to consist of reconnaissances to various villages in the interior. Before leaving Beikos most of the Indian ranks had visited the latest class of battleship as represented by the *Iron Duke*, *Royal Sovereign* and *Ramillies*, which were lying in the Bosphorus.

At the end of September orders were received for the Battalion to return to India. It embarked on H.T. *Eduard Woermann* on October 4th, disembarked at Karachi on October 21st, and arrived at Montgomery on October 29th, exactly six years after it had left Nowshera for active service in 1914. All Indian ranks were then granted two months' leave.

The Depot, which, in spite of the return of numbers of men from the 1st/152nd Punjabis, had now sunk to about 300, and was at once amalgamated with the Battalion. Major A. C. H. Trevor, who had returned from

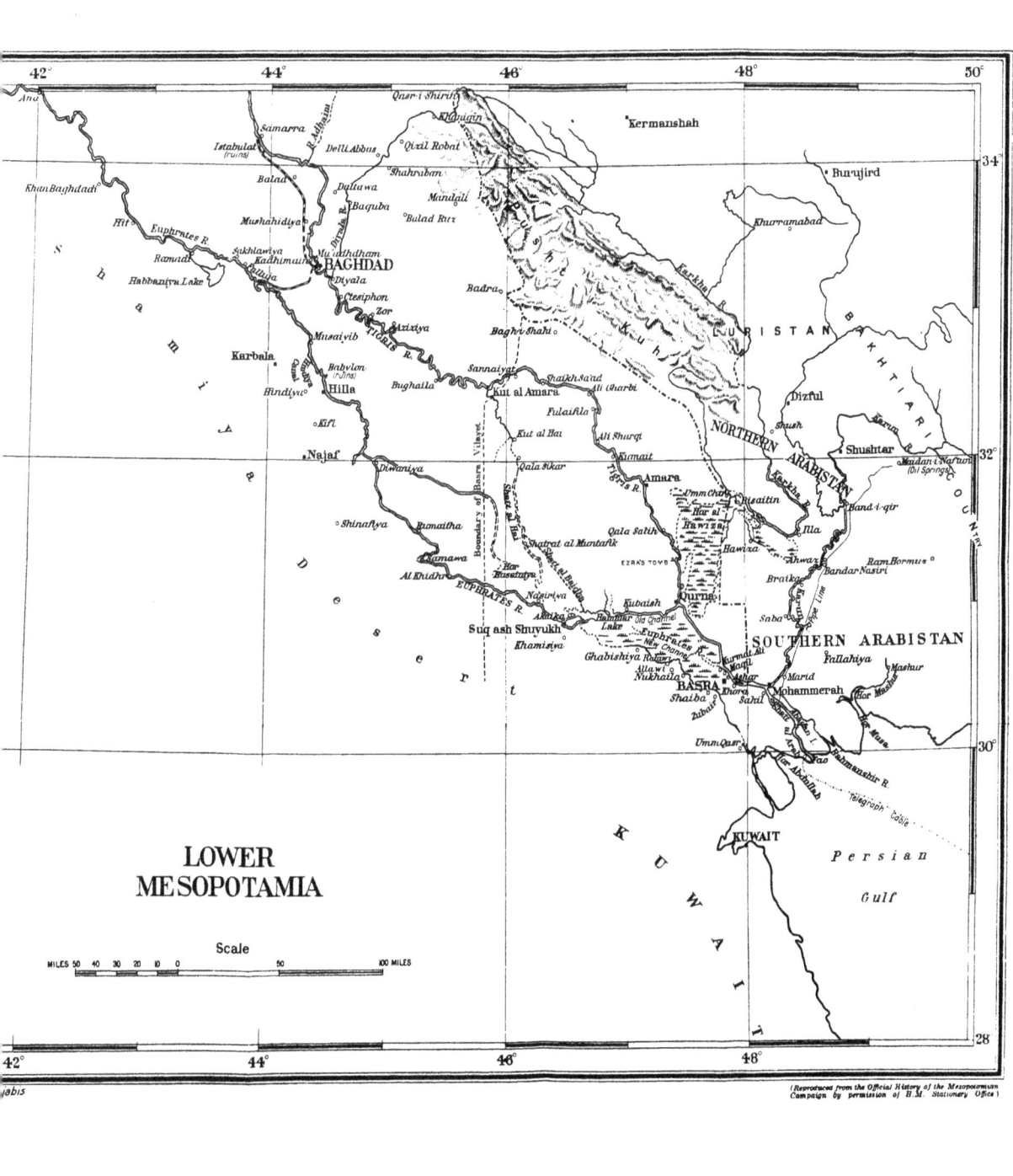

leave in January, 1920, was in command, and the presence of a pre-war officer was of the greatest value, especially in the allotment of war rewards of land and Jangi Inams, under which schemes about 180 ranks were granted rewards. The following Indian officers had been transferred to pension prior to the arrival of the Battalion in India :—,

Rai Sahib Janki Pershad, the head clerk (after fifty-four years' service, which so far as is known is a record for the Indian Army).

Subedar-Major and Honorary Captain Sakt Chand, Sirdar Bahadur.

Subedars Kehr Singh, Kishen Singh, Umar Khan, Jhanda Singh, Lal Mir and Sudama.

Jemadars Sher Singh, Nathu, Sher Baz, Firoz Khan, Lachhman Singh, Sawan Singh, Bhagat Singh and Faiz Ahmed.

Jemadar Narain Singh was transferred to the 2nd/74th Punjabis.

As regards the British officers, all the temporary commissioned and I.A.R. officers had been demobilized before the return of the Battalion to India. Of the officers shown in Appendix " J," only six were still with the Battalion on its return to India. Colonel Cummins left in December to assume officiating command of the Bombay District. He did not return again to the Battalion, as he was promoted to Major-General, and confirmed in the command of the Bombay District.

This ends the story of the work of the 24th during the Great War. It was a curious coincidence that the Regiment arrived back at its station in India in 1920, six years to a day after its departure on service from Nowshera in 1914. During those six years the 24th had an extremely varied career. The Regiment served in four theatres of war and formed part of, or was attached to, six separate divisions. The original battalion, moreover, suffered what is probably the worst fate which could have befallen a unit or an individual soldier during the Great War—namely that of being prisoners of war in the hands of the Turks.

It was, perhaps, therefore fitting, and certainly a satisfaction that the re-formed battalion should have spent its last months of service during the Great War period in the country, and close to the capital, of the nation, at whose hands its comrades had suffered gross ill-treatment.

All ranks, accordingly, thoroughly realized that the enemy nation against which the Regiment had been mainly employed, had suffered complete defeat.

APPENDICES

APPENDIX A.

British Officers borne on the Rolls of the 24th Punjabis in October, 1914.

* denotes killed ; † denotes wounded ; ‡ denotes died ; § denotes prisoner of war.

I. Proceeded on Service with the Battalion in October, 1914.

†Lieut.-Colonel S. H. Climo, D.S.O.	Commandant.
*†Major H. W. F. Cooke.	
*Major S. Morton.	
*Captain W. F. B. Edwards.	
*Captain G. Leslie-Smith.	
§†Captain A. B. Haig	Adjutant.
*Lieut. M. Birkbeck	Quartermaster.
*†Lieut. D. Hobart.	
†Lieut. C. C. Langhorne.	
*Lieut. E. S. Rind.	
Lieut. H. M. Pim.	
Captain R. C. Clifford, I.M.S.	Medical Officer.

II. Left at the Depot.

§Captain A. C. H. Trevor	Joined the Battalion in July, 1915.
*2/Lieut. W. H. L. Passy	Attached to 53rd Sikhs Frontier Force, February, 1916.

III. Officers Extra-Regimentally Employed in October, 1914.

§†Major H. A. V. Cummins	D.A.Q.M.G. Bombay District. Joined Battalion in July, 1915.
Major A. K. Rawlins, D.S.O.	With Imperial Service Troops. Commanded the Bikanir Camel Corps throughout the war.
Bt. Lieut.-Colonel A. Skeen	Instructor Staff College, Quetta. Proceeded to Gallipoli, 1915, and served on the Staff throughout the war. Promoted to Major-General, June, 1918.
*Captain E. H. Le M. Sinkinson	With Imperial Service Troops. Joined Battalion in July, 1915.
Captain H. M. Wilson	A.D.C. to G.O.C. Peshawar District. Transferred to Skinner's Horse, 1915.
‡Lieut. C. M. Thornhill	In France and Mesopotamia with 129th Baluchis and on Staff of Dehra Dun Brigade. Did not join Battalion in the field.

APPENDIX B.

Pre-War Regular Officers of Other Units who served with the 24th Punjabis.

*Lieut. H. C. Dillon	26th Punjabis	December, 1914—November, 1915.
Captain A. O. Sutherland	22nd Punjabis	August—November, 1915.
Captain Black	11th Rajputs	August—September, 1915.
§‡Captain C. A. Bignell	4th Rajputs	August, 1915. Died as prisoner of war.
Lieut.-Colonel Malcolm	31st Punjabis	October, 1916—February, 1917.
Lieut.-Colonel J. L. Furney	22nd Punjabis	February, 1917—December, 1919.
Major F. A. Magniac	22nd Punjabis	February, 1917—1918.
Captain G. W. Atkins, M.C.	25th Punjabis	February, 1917—1919.
‡Captain P. Conder	19th Punjabis	February, 1917—July, 1917.
Captain R. B. Deedes	31st Punjabis	1917-18. Commanded the Depot.
Captain C. F. Scroope	66th Punjabis	October, 1918—December, 1920. Subsequently permanently transferred to the 24th Punjabis.

APPENDIX C.

Regular Officers commissioned during the War who served with the 24th Punjabis.

	Date of Joining
Lieut. G. P. Troughton Dean	1915 (Depot)
Lieut. K. C. B. Dawes	1915 (Depot)
Lieut. C. J. Attfield	1916 (Depot)
Lieut. T. B. Yarrow	1917
Lieut. C. L. Sevenoaks	1917
Lieut. H. G. P. Stubbs	1917
Lieut. W. R. Hay	1917
Lieut. F. C. Barry	1918
Lieut. W. A. Colbourne	1918
Lieut. J. C. Cotton	1918
Lieut. P. E. C. Gwyn	1918
Lieut. C. H. Fison	1918
Lieut. C. Page	1918
Lieut. A. M. Barnes	1919
Lieut. C. Gault	1919
Lieut. A. P. Cunningham, M.C.	1919
Lieut. J. Exshaw	1919

APPENDIX D.

Officers of the I.A.R.O. who served with the 24th Punjabis.

	Date of Joining
2/Lieut. C. H. K. Phillips	December, 1914.
§2/Lieut. W. W. A. Phillips	December, 1914
*Lieut. J. C. Haverfield	May, 1915.
2/Lieut. F. W. Holland	May, 1915.
2/Lieut. A. J. McLellan	July, 1915.
*Lieut. G. P. Horst	July, 1915.
§2/Lieut. H. Browne	August, 1915.
2/Lieut. R. Hockey	August, 1915.
§Lieut. E. L. Duxbury	September, 1915.
§Lieut. H. E. Stapleton	September, 1915.
2/Lieut. W. G. L. Gilbert	December, 1915.
2/Lieut. J. D. Drew	January, 1916.
Lieut. K. McI. Kemp	April, 1917.
*Lieut. A. P. Algar	April, 1917.
*Lieut. A. I. Aymer	April, 1917.
2/Lieut. E. G. Evans	May, 1918.

APPENDIX E.

Officers who served at the Depot between 1918 and 1920.

	Date of Joining
Lieut. V. G. L. Prideaux	1917
Lieut. W. A. Dobney	1918
Lieut. Beasley	1918
Captain F. N. Hill	1918
Lieut. C. E. Penny	1918
Lieut. T. W. Carey	1918
Lieut. C. H. Buckingham	1918
Lieut. A. G. Millar	1918
2/Lieut. de Silva	1918
2/Lieut. C. A. Sampson	1918
2/Lieut. A. Shakell	1918
Captain Colquhoun	1920

Appendix F.

Casualties.

	Killed.	Died of Disease.	Wounded.
British Officers	14	3	6
Indian Officers	5	3	16
Indian Other Ranks (including followers)	188	204	517
Total	207	210	539

Grand Total ... 956

Notes.

(*a*) It has been difficult to arrive at absolutely accurate figures. The figures are based on casualty returns as given in War diaries checked as far as possible with the casualty returns of the Mesopotamia Expeditionary Force.

(*b*) The figures include casualties sustained by the Battalion in all theatres of war, but exclude those suffered by the Company of the 24th with the 1/152nd Punjabis in Palestine; and further exclude the figures of deaths from disease in Kut during April, 1916, which are not available.

(*c*) Figures under "Died of Disease, Indian Other Ranks," include 159 who died while prisoners of war in Turkey, but exclude numbers who died of disease in Mesopotamia in 1917-18.

(*d*) In the War Memorial at Basra are two plaques on which are inscribed the names of British Officers and Indian Officers and the total number of Indian Other Ranks, whose graves are not known. Under the heading "Mesopotamia" the figure of Indian Other Ranks is given as 179, and under "Turkey" as 153.

British Officers.

Killed :—

Major H. W. F. Cooke.
Major S. Morton.
Captain W. F. B. Edwards.
Captain E. H. Le M. Sinkinson.
Captain G. Leslie-Smith.
Lieut. M. Birkbeck.
Lieut. D. Hobart.
Lieut. E. S. Rind.
Lieut. H. C. Dillon (26th Punjabis).
Lieut. W. H. L. Passy.
Lieut. J. C. Haverfield, I.A.R.O.
Lieut. A. P. Algar, I.A.R.O.
Lieut. A. I. Aymer, I.A.R.O.
Lieut. G. P. Horst, I.A.R.O. (with Mekran Levy Corps).

Died of Disease :—

Captain C. A. Bignell (4th Rajputs).
Captain P. Conder (19th Punjabis).
Captain (A./Major) C. M. Thornhill, D.S.O., M.C.

Indian Officers.

Killed :—

Subadar Sahib Nur.
Subadar Sawan Singh, I.O.M.
Jemadar Sohan Singh, M.C.
Jemadar Muzaffar Hussain.
Jemadar Mula Singh.

Died of Disease :—

Jemadar Satiagar.
Jemadar Bhola Singh.
Jemadar Mohamed Afzal.

APPENDIX G.

Honours and Awards.

The following Honours and Awards were gained by all ranks of the 24th Punjabis:—

C.B. (1).
Lieut.-Colonel S. H. Climo, D.S.O.

C.M.G. (2).
Lieut.-Colonel H. A. V. Cummins. Lieut.-Colonel A. Skeen.

C.I.E. (1).
Lieut.-Colonel A. K. Rawlins, D.S.O.

C.B.E. (1).
Lieut.-Colonel A. K. Rawlins, D.S.O.

D.S.O. (2).
Lieut. C. M. Thornhill. Captain R. C. Clifford, I.M.S.

M.C. (10).
Captain H. M. Pim.
Captain C. M. Thornhill.
Captain R. C. Clifford, I.M.S.
Captain A. B. Haig.
Captain C. H. K. Phillips.
Captain G. P. Troughton Dean.
Captain C. L. Sevenoaks.
Lieut. A. P. Cunningham.
Jemadar Sohan Singh, I.O.M.
Subadar Gul Akbar, I.D.S.M.

Bar to M.C. (1).
Captain A. B. Haig.

Croix de Guerre (French.)
Captain C. M. Thornhill.

Croce de Guerra (Italian).
Havildar Bostan Khan.

Medaille Militaire (French).
Havildar Sawan Singh.

Medaille Barnatiesi Credinta (Rumanian).
Sepoy Zowarai, I.D.S.M.

Brevet Colonel (3).
Lieut.-Colonel S. H. Climo, C.B., D.S.O. Lieut.-Colone A. Skeen, C.M.G.
Lieut.-Colonel H. A. V. Cummins, C.M.G.

Promoted to Major-General (2).
Colonel S. H. Climo, C.B., D.S.O. Colonel A. Skeen, C.M.G.
(Both June 3rd, 1918.)

Order of British India (5).
Subadar-Major Sakt Chand.
Subadar Gul Akbar, M.C., I.D.S.M.
Subadar Sawan Singh, I.O.M.
Subadar Fateh Singh, I.O.M.
Subadar-Major Labh Singh.

Indian Order of Merit (16).

318 Sepoy Yarak.
4943 Lance-Naik Lal Singh.
4358 Lance-Naik Gosaun, I.D.S.M.
4812 Sepoy Parmodh Singh.
4974 Sepoy Gheba Khan.
3490 Sepoy Feroz Khan.
    Jemadar Sohan Singh.
4022 Sepoy Mangal Singh, I.D.S.M.

242 Sepoy Lachman Singh.
514 Lance-Naik Pal Singh, I.D.S.M.
4375 Havildar Sundar Singh.
4755 Naik Labh Singh, I.D.S.M.
    Jemadar Karam Ilahi.
    Subadar Ujagar Singh, I.D.S.M.
1289 Naik Bhag Singh.
699 Lance-Naik Kehr Singh.

Indian Distinguished Service Medal (42).

514 Lance/Naik Pal Singh, I.O.M.
405 Sepoy Vir Singh.
4909 Sepoy Labh Singh.
4866 Naik Sardar Khan.
4668 Naik Ulas Mir.
4755 Naik Labh Singh, I.O.M.
4510 Naik Kharak Singh.
474 Sepoy Khazan Singh.
4810 Lance/Naik Ganda Singh.
4650 Naik Haidar Khan.
709 Sepoy Sohnu.
39 Sepoy Lala.
131 Sepoy Ram Singh.
4487 Sepoy Gindu.
4950 Sepoy Siama.
4956 Sepoy Jiwan Singh.
544 Sepoy Yar Akhmad.
663 Sepoy Nawab Ali.
640 Sepoy Thakur Singh.
4301 Havildar Bhagwan Singh.
4417 Lance/Naik Hari Ram.

441 Sepoy Kishan Singh.
4874 Havildar Garbha.
120 Havildar Askar Khan.
2352 Sepoy Zawarai.
    Subadar Ujagar Singh, I.O.M.
230 Havildar Tehl Singh.
4022 Havildar Mangal Singh, I.O.M.
4552 Havildar Kesar Singh.
4703 Naik Bhagat Singh.
4754 Naik Kharak Singh.
1158 Sepoy Pal Singh.
930 Sepoy Kartar Singh.
370 Sepoy Pal Singh.
    Jemadar Pirthi Chand.
4358 Naik Gosaun, I.O.M.
383 Sepoy Lal Singh.
257 Sepoy Amar Singh.
4989 Sepoy Kishen Singh.
4505 Naik Lachman Singh.
922 Sepoy Labh Singh.
    Subadar Suba Ram.

Indian Meritorious Service Medal (27).

1798 C.H.M. Akbar Khan.
1372 Sepoy Hira Singh.
1680 Sepoy Latif Gul.
1875 Sepoy Malla Singh.
1584 Sepoy Hatib.
1273 Naik Jai Singh.
1003 Havildar Sher Ali.
4865 Havildar Lachman Singh.
792 C.Q.M.-Havildar Udham.
4970 Havildar Khushal Singh.
1034 Havildar Batan Khan.
345 Havildar Janta Singh.
171 Havildar-Major Gurdit Singh.
1561 Sepoy Nagib Ullah.

145 Sepoy Bhaji.
634 Sepoy Katha Singh.
663 Sepoy Nawab Ali, I.D.S.M.
4108 Havildar Bishan Singh.
492 Havildar (Clerk) Nanak Chand.
645 Sepoy Sawan Singh.
265 Naik Mangal Singh.
41 Havildar-Major Gul Azbar.
4580 C.H.M. (Clerk) Fakhar Din.
4058 Havildar Kahan Singh.
4847 Havildar Bela Singh.
4951 Naik Karam Singh.
711 Havildar Nadar Khan.

APPENDIX H.

Enlistments.

The total number enlisted in the 24th Punjabis between August 4th, 1914, and November 11th, 1918, was 3,465.

APPENDIX J.

The officers serving with the 24th Punjabis in the field on January 1st, 1919, were as follows:—

Commandant	Bt. Lieut.-Colonel J. L. Furney.
2nd-in-Command	Major G. W. Atkins, M.C.
"A" Company	Lieut. (A./Captain) C. H. K. Phillips, M.C.
	Lieut. G. Page.
2 Platoons P.Ms.	Subadar Shadam Khan.
	Jemadar Askar Khan, I.D.S.M.
2 Platoons Sikhs	Subadar Hakim Singh.
	Jemadar Ganda Singh, I.D.S.M.
"B" Company	Captain C. F. Scroope.
	Lieut. W. A. Colbourne.
2 Platoons Yusafzai	Subadar Sarfraz Khan.
	Jemadar Pir Dost.
2 Platoons Sikhs	Subadar Labh Singh (A./Subadar-Major).
	Jemadar Sher Singh.
"C" Company	Lieut. (A./Captain) G. P. T. Dean.
	Lieut. P. E. C. J. Gwyn.
2 Platoons Dogras	Subadar Suba Ram.
	Jemadar Shamsher Singh.
2 Platoons Sikhs	Subadar Wagar Singh.
	Jemadar Gurdit Singh.
"E" Company	Captain K. McI. Kemp.
	Lieut. H. C. Fison.
3 Platoons P.Ms.	Subadar Suba Khan.
1 Platoon Dogras	Jemadar Niamat Khan.
	Jemadar Garbha Ram, I.D.S.M.
Adjutant	Lieut. (A./Captain) H. G. P. Stubbs.
Jemadar Adjutant	Jemadar Lal Singh, I.O.M.
Quartermaster	Lieut. (A./Captain) T. B. Yarrow.
Jemadar Quartermaster	Jemadar Wadhawa Singh.
Transport Officer	Lieut. F. C. Barry.

www.ingramcontent.com/pod-product-compliance
Lightning Source LLC
Chambersburg PA
CBHW080406170426
43193CB00016B/2823